To Patti and Dave —
May you find in yourselves
and in each other a new
and fulfilling flow of love.

Eric Butterworth

Life Is for Loving

Life

Is for Loving

ERIC BUTTERWORTH

HARPER & ROW, PUBLISHERS

New York, Evanston, San Francisco, London

Designed by C. Linda Dingler

Library of Congress Cataloging in Publication Data

Butterworth, Eric.
  Life is for loving.
  Includes bibliographical references.
  1. Love (Theology) I. Title.
BV4639.B88   1973   248'.4   73–6326
ISBN 0–06–061268–1

To Olga
My true helpmate, with whom this book was
conceived, the concepts practiced, and the conti-
nuity polished . . . whose gems of love-wisdom
will be found liberally sprinkled through the
copy, and whose love and support will be
dynamically felt between the lines.

Contents

Introduction

"Another book about love! What more is there to say?" My answer to that is: With all the personal conflicts and frustrations and the world's wars and rumors of war, we obviously haven't had enough to say about love. Or perhaps we simply haven't understood what love is.

Has the word "love" become for most of us simply a meaningless cliché? We preach about love, we read love stories, and today there are dozens of "love" posters using formats that vary from the sensitive to the pornographic. But what does the word "love" mean? Semanticists tell us that no word has meaning—only people have meaning when they use the word. What, then, do we mean when we use the word "love"?

I have discovered a strange phenomenon in the words we use most often. Note the many words we use to describe a state of personal fullness: joyful, peaceful, beautiful, careful, cheerful, insightful, faithful, grateful, healthful, plentiful, successful, etc. If "love" is really the "greatest thing in the world," why have we never felt impelled to coin the word "loveful" (full of love)? Could this mean that we have never thought of the reality of love as an inner power—or of the possibility of being truly fulfilled in love?

After reading *Life Is for Loving* you may conclude that the word "loveful" should be a valid term. Perhaps you will even begin to use the term in salutations such as "Have a loveful day!" or, in a more meaningful way, in describing a person as being "beautiful and loveful." But, most important to our thesis, you will want to work for a self-evaluation that implies that you are full of the power of love—"I am a loveful person."

Let me warn you, *Life Is for Loving* will be extremely repetitious, for I am building on the theme that "love" is the very Genesis of the creation and the nature of the creative process in man. I have taken seriously the Scriptural text, "God is love," and that "man is created in the image-likeness of God." It must logically follow, then, that man is created in and of love. Love is man's true nature, whether he knows it or releases it or not.

Despite the weight of psychological teaching or human belief, love is *not* an emotion or sensual experience. It is *not* the plaything of human volition. Love is the action of a totally transcendent power and process within you. Therefore love does not begin in you and end in the one you love. It begins in a Cosmic Source, flows out through you, and goes on without end. This is not a concept that will come easily to your consciousness. It may take much meditation and serious study—which is the very reason why it will appear again and again throughout the book as an ever-recurring theme.

Most importantly: life is not for existing or "making do." Life is for loving and living abundantly, for you are, innately, a loveful person.

Prologue

Love is the foundation of the creative process, the root of the reality of the universe, and the very nature of the Infinite Power and Presence we call God. All things begin with love. Genesis says, "In the beginning God. . . ." But then John says, "God is love!" The Word is Love. Thus, paraphrasing John, "In the beginning was Love, and Love was with God, and Love was God." "And God said, Let us make man in our image, after our likeness. . . ." This image-likeness is the transcendent nature of creative love. "So God created man in his own image, in the image of God he created him." Thus it is that man is created in and of love. No matter how far he may stray from the root of reality into the circumference of living, it is always true in principle ("in the beginning . . .") that he is rooted and grounded in the allness of love. The chief work of man's life is always to "Call to remembrance" his true nature, which is created in the image and likeness of God who is love, and to get on with the business of life—which is for loving.

I. *From Love to Loving*

Let's talk about love! Better yet, let's practice being loving. There is no dearth of essays on love. In fact, man has written more extensively and articulately on the subject of love than any other area of life. Paul's 13th Chapter of I Corinthians is a classic work of scripture. Henry Drummond's *Love: The Greatest Thing in the World* is a classic of more modern times. And Erich Fromm's *The Art of Loving* has been read and studied by countless persons in our day. And yet, it must be said that love, in the particular emphasis that we are going to give it, is a relatively rare phenomenon in our society.

If we are honest we will admit that "love" has become a grand cliché. It has been called "a many splendored thing," but most of these splendors are abstract ideals, or even popular slogans such as, "Love makes the world go round." There is no word in the language that is used with more meanings than love, and most of them are unconsciously insincere in that they hide the true underlying motives and feelings. The brutal frankness of Charlie Brown is hilarious because it is so true to life: "I love all mankind—it's people I can't stand."

How easily we parrot the words, "Love will bring peace to the world and solve all problems of racial discrimination." However, as a word or concept, love cannot solve anything. The statement, "What the world needs now is love," is normally followed by a lengthy dissertation on the theme. But the world doesn't need sermons on love. It needs, rather, a new commitment to the activity of loving. We know how important love is to a child—not concepts of love, but a continuity of *tender loving care.*

One young girl left home in an effort to survive as a person after many years in a home totally devoted to Love. The parents were devotees of a religion that emphasized the power of Divine Love. It was the subject of much of their family conversation. Whenever the young girl had any kind of personal problem, her mother would say, "You go to your room and read this pamphlet on Divine Love." She said, "I got sick and tired of Divine Love. I wanted someone to talk lovingly to me, to be kind to me, to be interested in me. My mother seemed incapable of loving; she could only talk about love." This young girl became a member of the drug culture, the object of scorn and condemnation by another generation that gave its children everything—except the feeling of being loved.

Unless we understand what love is and how it works, to talk about "love is the answer," or to tell people "if you just love enough you will solve every problem," can well promote hypocrisy and sham, which are greater deterrents to learning to love than outright hostility. If I tell you that I don't like you one little bit, at least you know right away where I stand. I am being honest and you can deal with me accordingly. But if I tell you that I love you, the knowledge of love being what it is, you can and perhaps you should be suspicious, or at least puzzled.

One of the fundamental problems in understanding love, in seeking to know and experience the power of love, is what Erich Fromm calls our "marketplace orientation." We use love as a motivation for stimulating consumer demand for a variety of products. Someone recently referred to Valentine's Day as "I love Hallmark Day." In other words, if we really love, if we "care enough to send the very best," we will buy this brand of greeting cards.

Love is so often weighed in the balance of *things.* "If he loved me he would give me that fur coat." "He must love her a great deal to give her so much." "He doesn't love much or he would do more." Parents expect their children to love them as repayment for all the care and expense they have been: "After all I have done for you, you owe me a lot of love." This gives rise to a continuing process of trying to evidence love by gifts, baubles, or money. And the sad thing is that these things do not reveal love, but its complete absence.

William Butler Yeats comments on man's loss of freedom. He says it is because we have turned the table of values upside down, believing that the root of reality is not in the center but somewhere in the whirling circumference. Life for most persons is almost completely exterior-oriented. We have been conditioned to believe that we come into life empty and go forth into the world to be filled. We go to school to get knowledge. We go to church to get religion. We go into the marketplace to get money and security. And we look to certain special people for love. Thus, love is outer-centered and other-motivated. It is thought of as an object rather than a faculty. If someone gives us love, then we will be able to love. Love comes natural to us when we find the right person to love, or to be loved by. Or so we reason.

Life for most persons is a long quest for love, which becomes a quest for objects of love. The most sordid and depraved lives are really crying out, "Won't someone please love me?" And yet, intuitively we know that love is an inner power and not an object, and that our need is to love and not just to find someone to love us. Within every person is a hunger and thirst to *be* love, to express love, to let the Infinite Power of Love flow through him.

A little eight-year-old girl in a Pennsylvania orphanage was shy and unattractive. She was regarded as a problem by her teachers. The director was seeking some pretext for getting rid of her. They had an ironclad rule that any communication from a child in the institution had to be approved before it could be mailed. One day the little girl was observed stealing down to the main gate where she reached out through the bars and tucked a letter onto the branch of a low-hanging tree. The director hurried down to the gate. Sure enough, the note was clearly visible, a clear violation of the rules. She pounced upon it, tore open the envelope, and read: "To anybody who finds this: I love you."

Modern psychology has misled people with its insistence that "the greatest need of man is to be loved." We have been taught to think of love as a commodity rather than a divine process. We have supposed that our lives lack love because we have not been loved. How easy it is to conclude that all the problems of our life have come about because of a father who mistreated us, or a mother who did not love us.

We need to redefine, or at least "un-define," this thing called love. We have accepted the Biblical statement, "God is love," as if love were a particular commodity that God sent down into life "from above." Actually, it is likely that the statement was more a description of what God is than what He does. Perhaps it was saying that God is like a diamond with a multitude of facets. Like saying: The sun is round. The sun is red. The sun is light. The sun is heat.

It may be said that God is Life, God is Intelligence, God is Power —and God is Love. But again, all this is simply abstract generalization unless and until we can say, "Whatever else God is, God is me. Not that I am all of God, but that I am that something that I call God as it is expressing itself *as* me. God is Life and I am that Life manifesting as my body temple. God is Intelligence, and I am that Intelligence in the form of the wisdom of my mind. God is Power, and I am that Power in the form of my strength and creativity to build and shape. God is Love, and I am that Love expressing in and through and *as* my loving heart." Thus, it is not "love" that is the great need in the life of persons —it is *loving*. We need to sing with St. Augustine, "I am in love with loving."[1] We need occasionally to return from the circumference of our life to the root of our being where we remember that "God created man in his own image, in the image of God he created him" (Gen. 1:27). Of course this can become little more than a cliché. The need is to personalize it: "God created *me* in His image—and God is love." Note the logical implication of this. Each of us is created in and of love. God loves us. God is love in us. Each of us is the very activity of love. We have all the love we need to love everyone and everything, for everyone and everything are also created in and of love. To love someone is not giving him a commodity. It is simply saluting the reality of him, celebrating the unity of life. It is love within us uniting with love within him.

Goethe suggests that we would not be able to see the sun if the eye were not of a sunny nature. How could the Godlike delight us, he asks, if the power of God did not already exist within us? In other words, if we were not made in and of love, how could we have a yearning for love? If we have a feeling of love for another, it is because we have to that degree felt a sense of love within ourselves. We have loved that person through loving ourselves. There is no other way to truly express love except through self-love.

Take a moment to reflect on this: You cannot give love to anyone, and no one can give love to you. You can be loving, which will create an environment in which others may find it easy to radiate and express love—and thus be loving to you. Love is not a commodity to give, but a process through which you touch and express your own deeper nature. Love, then, is not the plaything of the emotions or senses, but the action of divine law.

Our capacity to love is directly dependent upon our ability to love ourselves with a mature self-love. Love is not something to get from people or even from God. For we are already created in and of love. Nor is it something we can ever lack. "I have loved you with an everlasting love" (Jer. 31:3). Love is the reality of our total self which we can frustrate or express. Unless we realize this truth, we may go on indulging in the romantic myth that "someday love will happen to me." Love has never "just happened" to anyone. People spend years of their lives trying to "find" love. But love is not to be found. It consists not in *finding* the right person, but in *becoming* the right person.

There has been much confusion in the Judaeo-Christian religion about the injunction, "Love thy neighbor." Because we have not really understood *love* or how to love a neighbor, this has been little more than a pious platitude or an impossible utopian prescription for the millennial future, an inert truth mumbled by people on Sabbath days and then promptly put back into the "six-day closet of unconcern." There is a Hebrew construction that can only be rendered archaically in English as "love *to* your neighbor," which means, "act lovingly toward him." This is the intent of the commandment. Not *love* him, but *be loving*. To "love him" deals with something you give him or something you do to him. *Being* loving deals more with your attitude, your level of perception, the way you see him.

Jesus made the commandment more meaningful when He said, "You shall love your neighbor *as yourself*" (Mark 12:31). You cannot really know and love another person unless you know and love yourself. Loving yourself is knowing what you are and rejoicing in it. Loving your neighbor is accepting what he is, which is made possible only as you accept what you are.

When you love yourself, you are secure and "within-dependent." You can face the changes in the world without threat. If you do not love yourself, you are not centered in the reality of yourself which *is* love. You are not letting yourself BE love. You are dependent for security on whether some other person acts lovingly toward you. In this consciousness every change in people and every changing condition is a threat that triggers in you a reaction of hate or resistance.

While riding in an elevator in a Spokane hotel, Bayard Rustin was ordered by a white man to lace up his shoes. Without objection or hesitation, he did as he was ordered. The man then handed him a tip. Rustin refused, saying, "Oh, I didn't do it for money. I assumed you really needed help." The man was extremely embarrassed and then apologetic. He invited Rustin to come to his room where they had a meaningful exchange on the subject of human relations.

You may say, "But I could never act like that!" It is not easy. It takes great inner strength which comes only from feelings of self-respect and mature self-love. The man obviously had a poor regard for himself, and that was the root of his discrimination. Rustin could treat the man lovingly without offense simply because the act of obvious discrimination was no threat to his security. He was established in the reality of his own being, which was love. Thus he could easily love his neighbor as himself, for he easily loved and respected himself.

Note that Bayard Rustin had a choice. He could have taken offense and then reacted in hostility and anger. But in that case he would have revealed a lack of self-respect. Or, as he did, he could simply *be* what he knew himself to be—a creature centered in the love of the Infinite which was adequate to help and heal any situation. No one would have criticized him if he had chosen the way of anger, for that is the way of the world. However, the wise man will always ask himself, "Why should I let another person determine how I am going to act?" The apostle Paul had often faced this kind of choice, thus it was from his own painful experience that he urged us not to let the world around us squeeze us into its own mold, but rather to let God remold our minds from within. Every one of us has a choice many times a day whether to react to situations in human consciousness, or, as Meister Eckhart might say, to let God be God in you.

Jesus carried the process even further when He said, "You have heard that it was said, 'You shall love your neighbor and hate your enemy.' But I say to you, Love your enemies and pray for those who persecute you, so that you may be sons of your Father who is in heaven" (Matt. 5:43). If we think that love is a commodity, something that we give to the person, then we are going to wonder if he is worthy of the gift. We may say, "But he is an enemy. He is not deserving of my love." However, if we realize that "God is Love and I am that Love expressing *as* me," then we will know that we experience the ISness of God's love only to the degree that we let this Love process move through us in our attitudes, our manners, and our actions.

The enemy may not deserve your love, but the overriding question is, "Do you deserve your love?" Jesus said, "Love . . . that you may be sons. . . ." You cannot afford *not* to be loving. For it is in loving that you activate the love process and thus open yourself to being loved from within. If you have an enemy, you have enmity, which is a state of consciousness in which you are frustrating your love potential.

An Egyptian ruler was once criticized because he did not destroy his enemies taken prisoner in battle. He replied, "Do I not destroy my enemies when I love them?" This ruler was not just parroting platitudes, but practicing the universal principle of love. He was not just saying, "Love will solve the war!" He was acting lovingly toward his enemies, and thus dissolving the warring states of his own consciousness.

Of course, Jesus is dealing with a love that is "inner-centered." This is transcendental love. It is not the kind of love for a person that remains as long as he is lovable. Shakespeare says truly, "Love is not love which alters when it alteration finds."[2] Outer-centered love may say, "I loved him with all my heart, but after what he did to me, I hate him with a passion." But this is not true love. It is what Fromm calls "symbiotic attachment." Inner-centered love can see a man lying drunk in the gutter as one who, in his way, is trying to find his lost treasure even as the one who is kneeling in ecstasy at the altar. It always responds to the appearance of weakness or even sin in others with the attitude, "Neither do I condemn you . . ."

Jesus said, "This is my commandment, that you love one another . . ." (John 15:12). This, again, means "that ye are loving to one another." You are not really getting the message of Truth unless you are loving, kind, thoughtful, tender, accepting people *as* people, as they are, and not just as your prejudices cause you to think they should be. Life can only be fully lived when you understand certain underlying spiritual principles. But you are not really living abundantly or creatively because you can recite a lot of definitions of Divine Love, or because you can talk easily about love as the key to world peace or converse in high-sounding platitudes such as "the brotherhood of man."

The important thing is: How do you deal with the people you pass on the street? Do you treat the janitor or garage mechanic or salesperson as an equal or as if he belonged to an inferior breed. Thoreau said that he could call no man charitable who forgets that the persons who work for him or with him are made of the same human clay as himself. To put it simply: Move from love platitudes to loving attitudes—and actions.

In all human relations it is good to begin with the principle that people are innately wonderful and beautiful—and *love-full*. It may be hard to see, for they may not see it in themselves. But people are real even beyond their superficiality. With practice, you will find that you can look *through* them instead of just *at* them. You will salute the divinity within them and celebrate love as the one great reality in which you both live and move and have being. Why take the trouble? Because you *do* live in the world, and because your own peace of mind and health of soul are totally dependent upon the relationships you establish with the world "out there."

The principle of love is dynamic. Certainly love can change the world and it can change you. But it can only do so if you take the principle into the laboratory and roll up your sleeves. You learn to speak by speaking. You learn to walk by walking. You learn to work by working. And you learn to love by loving. There is no other way.

Study love. Meditate on the love idea and the whole process of loving. Here is a good exercise: Take a love walk. Make contact with every person you pass—but in a loving way. Look beyond the appearances to see from the consciousness of love, which will enable you to behold and see the lovable within even the most sordid character. This is an excellent way to sharpen your consciousness of love as the greatest power in your life. It will also be an effective means of letting a world of peace and order begin with you. But more than this, it is the best possible technique for creating an umbrella of the "protecting love of God." No harm could ever befall you if you were totally in the consciousness of love. And your consciousness of love is never complete, no matter how many love-affirmations you may be rehearsing, unless you are in the attitude and action of loving.

By nature, every person is generous and loving, but he may well have frustrated this divine impulse in subtle ways. In times of great crises when people are thrown together in the common bond of fear or insecurity, as in war or an earthquake, it is often the subject of conversation how loving and mutually helpful people suddenly become. There is no logical explanation for the phenomenon other than that people are really this way beneath the façade of their own faulty self-esteem. But no matter what a person is or is not, no matter what he has done or may have left undone, everyone yearns to renounce his status as a parasite upon life and to become a patron of life. Most of all he hungers to give love to the world. He may not understand the working of love; that God always loves him and *is* love within him, that he is created in and of love and thus he always has enough love to meet any situation. He may even tear at the world like a child tearing at a Raggedy-Ann doll. But his urge for love and for loving is always present as an explanation for his hungers and drives and also as a key to his potential for growth and achievement.

It is sad that religious organizations have placed the emphasis upon charity as the way to apply love. The word "charity" comes from the Latin word "caritas," which means "to love," or more literally, "to care." But as the word is used in our times, it has come to be almost completely divorced from the idea of love. The emphasis is upon materiality. Thus you may give to the starving Biafrans or war-torn Bangladesh, or you may even organize charities and give parties and bazaars to raise money for "relief"—and still never take the step from *love* to *loving*, from sympathy to empathy.

Francis J. Gable tells of an experience in his own life when he was a traveling salesman. It was one of those rare revelations of transcendent significance that came from following a flash of inner guidance. He was passing hurriedly through a train station bent on catching the 8:40 to Chicago, when he was confronted by a crippled beggar sitting with his pencils and cup. Following his charitable instinct he dropped a coin in the cup and hurried on past. Suddenly, a few steps farther on, he stopped short and pondered the significance of his act. He turned and addressed the man, saying, "I want to apologize to you. I treated you like a beggar, but you are really a merchant." At that he stooped and took a pencil and then hurried on to catch his train.

It was a spontaneous thing, but with implications much more far-reaching than at the time he realized. He was traveling through that same station two years later. As he passed this same spot he heard a voice calling out, "Hey mister!" He turned and recognized this same crippled man, now seated on a high stool, working as the proprietor of a bustling newspaper stand. The man said, "You probably don't remember me, but I will never forget you. You treated me as a person, and for the first time in my life I realized that I could make something of myself. I have now found a way to be self-supporting, but, most of all, I now have self-respect." In a moment Gable turned from love to loving, from charity to involvement—and a life was transformed.

Yes, let's talk about love—but let us not stop there. Let us resolve to practice being loving. Let us remember that love is not finding the right person to love or be loved by. It is being the right person *of* love. And then let us meditate long on the realization that we are created in and of love, that love is the one reality of our life, and that there is always enough love to go around—if we are willing to turn it on by being loving.

Dostoevsky, in his *The Brothers Karamazov*, writes: "Love all of God's creation, the whole and every grain of sand in it. Love every leaf, every ray of God's light. Love the animals, love the plants, love everything.

If you love everything, you will perceive the divine mystery of things. Once you perceive it, you will begin to comprehend it better every day. And you will come at last to love the whole world with an all-embracing love."[3] Then, with Charlie Brown, you will declare, "I love all mankind." But unlike him, you will add, "And I love all people as I love myself." I am loving to everyone whose path crosses mine, even if he unfairly or unjustly treats me, not because he deserves my love but because I do—for life is for loving. And I affirm as my own celebration of life: I am a channel for the expression of the Infinite Love of God.

2. *Love and Forgiveness*

"Oh, if I could just know that God would or could forgive me!" As a counselor I have observed this as an almost universal direct or implied cry. Implicit in this torment of soul is the feeling of living with the stain of personal sin and under the burden of the condemnation of self and of God.

The love of God has been presented as being capricious. The Old Testament God loves and hates, He creates and destroys. His wrath and anger at times is frightening to behold. What we have not taken into account is that these writings reflect the fact that the early Hebrews were only a little removed from the belief in many pagan deities, and thus their concept of the "One God" did not always reflect the purity in which Moses gave it to them. Fortunately, there is an occasional glimpse of the reality of God as principle, such as in Jeremiah: "I have loved you with an everlasting love" (Jer. 31:3). This is the principle that we should use as the basis for all inquiries into the reasons for love or its seeming absence in human perversity. There is a creative intention of love within us at all times. We are always *in* love, we are always loved, and we always have enough love within us to deal with any and all relationships and experiences in the world.

When, then, do we feel the lack of love? Why do we have the plaguing hunger to be loved? Whence comes the sense of evil and guilt? What, then, is sin, and how do we forgive sin—our own and that of others? And, most of all, how can we know that God loves us, and that

He can and will forgive our wrongdoing?

The only reason for the feeling of being unloved is that we have been conditioned to an exterior orientation of love. We have grown up thinking that love is something that comes to us and from us, rather than that which flows through us from an inward source that is inexhaustible. We are like ants in a sugar mill, who sit on vast mounds of sugar and yet hold out their tentacles in a desperate attempt to catch a grain or two as it flies by. With boundless pools of love within us, we look hungrily into the faces of persons passing by for some evidence of love. The love-starved person is not a victim of circumstances as we have erroneously supposed, but a victim of his own unconscious refusal to let the activity of love flow through him, loving himself, and thus radiating a love that builds on a secure and mature self-love. The hunger for love that is so common to all persons is the ceaseless urge to "open out a way whence the imprisoned splendor may escape."[1] However, misreading the call, we tend to go searching in the world for that which can only be found within ourselves.

The dictionary defines sin as "the transgression of divine law." The transgression is in acting out images of frustration and limitations despite the fact that we are created totally in the image and likeness of God, who is love. The sin is being out of harmony with the reality of our own being. Sin is not knowing our inherent divinity and thus living a lie by acting as if our humanity were the reality of us. When man doesn't know his divinity, when he doesn't know the depth of his own innate goodness, when he doesn't know that he is a wonderful and *loveful* expression of God, he does a lot of things that are the result of the frustration of his potentiality. The result is what is called *evil*, which may be defined as "the concealment of the good."

All so-called "sin" and "evil" arise from a lack of the feeling of love and being loved. Not understanding this, we have tried to correct evil with punishment and vindictiveness. Both religious and political systems have often failed to realize that "you have not converted a man because you have silenced him." The threat of "an eye for an eye" may inhibit the evil act, but it does nothing to correct the supposed evil power, which is simply a pent-up force of spiritual energy that is being frustrated and perverted. Feelings of guilt arise from the misreading of an intuitive sense of the Allness of our love, and from an unconscious feeling that the darkness of our behavior is the result of the self-concealment of the light that eternally glows within us, "the spark which a man may desecrate but never quite lose." The guilt feeling is the call to "arise and sin no more," to turn on the light of transcendental love, to remove the mask of self-limitation and reveal the image of our true self, created in the divine image of love.

"But I still feel guilty," you may insist. "How can I find the forgiveness of God for my sins?" Turn again to the principle: "I have loved you with an everlasting love." The problem is that we have created God in our image-likeness, and thus we see the Divine as having the capricious moods of the human. Sin is our own frustration of inherent goodness, cutting ourselves off from the activity of God, the power of love that is constant. Paul says, "The wages of sin is death" (Rom. 6:23). But this simply means that if we cut the light circuit we have darkness, or if we prune the branch from the tree it immediately experiences progressive deterioration. We are not punished *for* our sins but *by* them.

If we fix a rubber band around our index finger, in a few minutes the finger will redden and swell and finally turn blue from lack of circulation. Before very long it will reach the danger point with serious deterioration setting in if the band is not released. Now, the reddened finger is not caused by the wrath of the life force in the body. It is simply the natural result of shutting off that force. And the life force in the body will not hold anything against the finger because there is no flow. The very moment we restore the flow of nourishing blood by removing the band, forgiveness is instantaneous. Life flows into the finger and circulation resumes normally.

Habakkuk reflects this principle of God's everlasting love for man when he says, "O Lord . . . Thou . . . art of purer eyes than to behold evil" (Hab. 1:13). Religious dogma to the contrary, God knows nothing of sin, of want, of lack. Does the principle of mathematics know anything about your mistake if you write two plus two equals five? Does electricity know anything about your darkened home if you have the circuits turned off? The tragedy would be if God did know sin. For if

God knew sin, He would be a sinner. What Mind knows, Mind must be. God is love, a principle and process that is love in you and that loves you totally and changelessly. God is not a person who loves you if you love Him, who loves you when you are good and hates you when you are bad, or who loves some persons more than others. Love is an attribute of Divine Mind, the idea and force of universal unity. It is the power that unites and binds in divine harmony the universe and everything in it—including you and me. Thus by principle we are bound in oneness with the Allness of Love. And the principle knows no caprice; it can never love us less, nor lessen its inexorable force.

How, then, do we find the forgiveness of God? How can we find freedom from our feelings of guilt? The plain truth is: God does not, cannot, hold less than love for us no matter what we have done or have left undone. Startling as it may seem, God does not forgive sin, God *cannot* forgive sin. To forgive sin He must be conscious of sin. To be conscious of sin must involve a judgment. Judgment is a frustration of divinity. Jesus said, "Judge not, that you be not judged" (Matt. 7:1). Thus, if God judges, He must be undivine.

God cannot forgive sin, for there is no judgment of wrong in Divine Mind. How do we get electricity to forgive us for the break in the circuitry? How do we get the life force in the body to forgive us for shutting off its flow with the rubber band? By turning the switch—by removing the restricting band. Life can never be less than life, and electricity can never be less than electricity. And, God can never be less than God. God is love even when we are filled with hatred, even when we are angry and bitter. But the very moment we release our bitterness, rise above our guilt, stop feeling sorry for ourselves, is the moment we let God, who has always loved us with an everlasting love, *be* God in us, *be* love in us. We may feel a wonderful sense of freedom and healing. We may sing, "God has forgiven me for my sins, praise be to God!" But what God has *done*—God has always *been* within us. We prodigals in the "far country" of separation have suddenly come to ourselves. Our indwelling Father stirs mightily within us, saying, in effect, "Let us eat and make merry, for you were dead and are now alive. Be assured, wherever you are I am your Father, and all that is mine is yours."

Jesus combined the forgiveness of others with the forgiveness of God. He knew that when we judge others we bind ourselves in a restricting judgment of self. Our bitterness and hatred and unforgiveness of others tightens the band in consciousness that shuts us from the constancy of God's healing love. So Jesus said in His model prayer, "Forgive us our debts, as we also have forgiven our debtors" (Matt. 6:12). This does not suggest a bargain. God makes no deals. It means that we must give to receive, and loose and let go of indignation if we would experience a loosening of the restrictions in our own life. When we get the idea of the principle of the constancy of God's love, it begins to make logical sense.

Of course, there is nothing logical about the feelings of human consciousness as Peter reveals when he asks, "Lord, how often shall my brother sin against me, and I forgive him? As many as seven times?" He is irked at people and their insensitivity to such spiritual ideals. He is saying, "But you can't go on forgiving people. How much can a person take?" Jesus replied, "I do not say to you seven times, but seventy times seven" (Matt. 18:21). In other words, if you want light in the room, you must turn on the switch and keep it on—or you will have to sit in darkness. Again we are dealing with law and not caprice.

We may feel that forgiving persons who have despitefully used us is too much to expect of us, and that we have good reason for turning off the light of love and a perfect right to our indignation. This is all very well in the logic of the human mind, but it omits the principle. Man is a spiritual being, created in and of love, with the "same Mind that was in Christ Jesus." Man is divine as Jesus was divine. But the power and privilege that goes with our divinity is only ours when we act the part. The difference between Jesus and us is not that He was created under a special dispensation, but that He acted constantly at the level of His divinity while we act much of the time at the level of our humanity.

If we judge the wrongs of others, then we will have to forgive them. Our judgment binds us to a restrictive flow of Divine Love. Thus, the forgiveness of others depends upon self-forgiveness. For when we see limitation, we are seeing from a limited perspective, which is a sense of limitation in ourselves. One teacher used to say, "Father, forgive me for expecting in the human that which is found only in the divine." If we relate to others as human creatures, there is bound to be the subconscious expectancy of human limitations. Our view of them will be prejudiced. Don't we say, "That's about what I expected from that character"? The sin, then, is really in the eye of the beholder. And the forgiveness of sin must come through understanding—not through setting things right but through seeing them rightly. Thus, forgiveness is removing the scales from our eyes. It is right-seeing leading to perfect understanding.

This approach to the forgiveness of sin may seem to imply a Pollyanna attempt to sweep all the evils of the world under the rug. The absolutist often says, "There is no evil." But this can be terribly misleading. Of course there is evil and there is sickness and there is pain and suffering —as anyone may see for himself if he walks through the halls of a hospital or sits for an hour or two in a big city police station. Evil is the concealment of good, caused by the frustration of the potentiality for good in many persons. There *is* a lot of good being concealed and a lot of God's love being restricted, resulting in an awful lot of perversity and inhumanity to man.

The truth is: There is no evil as a separate power, even as darkness is not of itself a power opposed to light. There is only one power, the power of God, the healing, harmonizing power of transcendent love. If we are in human consciousness, judging by appearances, it is not easy to forgive. Perhaps on this level it is impossible to forgive. The first step, then, is to "turn the other cheek," to turn to the other side of our nature from the human to the divine, and thus to judge not according to "appearances, but judge with right judgment" (John 7:24). This means to stop "seeing in part," with all the separation and deterioration, and see wholeness, see Allness, see with eyes of love. That doesn't come easy, especially when it is we or ours who have been hurt by the evil actions of others. It is difficult even in the minor slights of life, and when it comes to wrongs that end in tragedy, the way of forgiveness is a hard road—but a necessary one.

In World War II a young German Secret Service man summoned a

Jew, any Jew, to his deathbed to beg forgiveness. The young Jew came into the room, heard out the story of the man plagued with the collective guilt of the Nazis, and then got up without a word and walked out. This young Jew survived the war and became the best known tracker of former Nazi executioners, the "Eichmann hunter," Simon W. Wiesenthal. His experience with the dying SS man is still with him. Several years ago he wrote the story in detail and invited forty or fifty prominent people to say what they would have done in his place. Some replied that they would have forgiven the man; many stated that they could not have done so.

Wiesenthal insists that in Judaism one cannot forgive wrongs done to other people, and that in the case of the Nazi crimes against the Jews they would never forgive. He says the call for forgiveness is absolutely hopeless! It does seem, however, that the question is much on his mind; almost as if he hopes someone could convince him of the importance of letting go.

Let's not judge Wiesenthal too harshly. We can understand his bitterness and confusion, and that of most Jews, especially those who may have been directly or indirectly involved in those times. But this is an opportunity to see the ideals of love and forgiveness in their most serious context. Someone said recently, relative to this experience of the Jews, "It is too serious a matter to forgive!" However, when we consider the spiritual law involved—and the needs of modern Israel, it is too serious a matter not to forgive.

It is the same with the black people and the prevailing view of some that the white people owe them a kind of reparation for the long history of slavery and segregation and mistreatment. And it may be seen in the family whose young child has been struck down on the street by a drunken driver, and in all the many cases where tragedy has been caused by negligence or by willful intent. However the law remains: FORGIVE AND YOU WILL BE FORGIVEN. We cannot endure without love, and there is no other way to the return of healing, comforting, harmonizing love than through total and complete forgiveness. If we want freedom and peace and the experience of love and being loved, we must let go and forgive and permit the activity of God to flow.

Of course, it goes without saying that we cannot and should not forgive a wrong while it is being committed; for that would not really be forgiving but condoning and supporting the wrong. Affix a steel band around a growing pumpkin and suddenly the whole life process within the pumpkin is geared toward bursting the band. The band is a limitation, and life cannot condone limitation. However, once the band is broken, or in another instance when a great rock is split asunder to allow an acorn to give birth to the giant tree, there is no forgiveness necessary for no judgment was made. If an evil act is being perpetrated on the life or person of a friend or loved one, obviously the act must be corrected. But once the act has ceased, we must forgive and let go; cleansing ourselves of bitterness or enmity. We may protest, "But the evil one does not deserve our love." Perhaps not, but the important question again is, do you deserve your love? If you remove the band of evil from the experience of another, it profits little if you then affix the band around yourself. That is precisely what you do when you harbor unforgiveness and thoughts of revenge. We should condemn the act, but forgive the actor. The crime is wrong and is a band to be broken, but the criminal is a divinity in disguise, a spiritual being to be awakened and reclaimed.

There are those who say that the criminal acts of men prove that human nature is evil. However, it is not human nature, but human *nurture* that is the problem. No one is born with criminal tendencies, or even with unloving thoughts. In every case it could be said that someone taught a child. While we go about trying to achieve vengeance, or redress or satisfaction, we are creating a whole new wave of "human nurture." The furor over the legality of "capital punishment" needs to be considered in this light. To take a life for a life that has been taken is an attempt to stop crime by committing more crime. A society that engages in or condones capital punishment can never achieve peace or even a modicum of "law and order" because it carries a millstone around its neck.

The one thing that unites all the great world religions is the emphasis that is given to love and nonresistance. We may find it hard to understand Jesus' directive to pray for enemies and to turn the other cheek.

And it is just not common sense to return to the person who does us wrong, the protection of our ungrudging love, as the Buddha commanded. But it is the uncommon sense of spiritual law. In every religion the law is the same: In the beginning . . . love! This means the principle is love. Love is the answer, the cure, and the healing therapy. The person who does wrong acts out of a frustration of the power and process of love in his life. It may seem to be perfectly normal to fight fire with fire and to meet his act with condemnation and hatred. But this is the stuff of which wars are made, and wars are never won. They are only ended in fatigue, even if one side claims a victory. The cause of the war, the unloving thoughts or actions, have not been diminished by the fatigue. They have simply been restricted with further bands of steel. If there is ever to be peace it can only come through love and forgiveness, which could have come in the first place before the tragic loss of human life.

Holding unforgiveness and responding with war or retaliation or a "punishment to fit the crime" is acting as though man is an isolated, separate creature; as if existence is not one and harmonious, but a chaos of competition and strife. It means that we are quite separate from our fellow man and can injure him, rob him, or hurt or destroy him, without any damage to ourselves. It means further that the more we take from other people the more we have for ourselves, and the more we consider our own interests and are indifferent to the welfare of others, the better off we are. And it follows that it pays others to treat us the same way. If all this be true, then the world is a jungle, and sooner or later the world must destroy itself by its own inherent weakness.

However, the *good news* of all the great mystic teachers of the ages is that there is a unity of life in which all persons are created in and of love, all are immersed in the same dynamic flow of infinite love, life, and wisdom. And all are given the choice: Know the truth and be free, or frustrate your potential and walk in darkness. We may act out the glorious role of divinity, or we may frustrate our potential for creative love and act out a self-image of the beast.

This gives rise to the concept of the personalization of the beastliness of man in the form of the Devil. It is the great "cop-out" of history. How easy it is to blame all the evil acts and intentions on the influence of

Satan. The Aquarian Gospel gives an interesting insight on the subject: "The only devil from which man must be redeemed is self, the lower self. If man would find his saviour he must look within; and when the demon self has been dethroned, the Saviour, Love, will be exalted to the throne of power. . . . The devil and the burning fires are both the works of man, and none can put the fires out and dissipate the evil one, but the man who made them both."[2] Thus, there is nowhere to look but within ourselves if we would find the cause of the evil experience or the way to its correction. "Forgive and you will be forgiven."

No, forgiveness of certain extreme acts of commission or omission is not easy. Unfortunately, continued unforgiveness is rationalized in Christianity as "righteous indignation." But righteous or unrighteous, it is still holding the nettle to our breast. There is a story of two Hindu priests on a long walking trip. They came to a woman in distress who was unable to cross a river. Despite the priestly vow not to touch a woman, one of the priests took pity on her and carried her over on his shoulders. For miles thereafter the second priest berated the first for breaking his vows. Finally, the first priest said, "My friend, I carried the damsel only across the stream and I promptly put her down; but you have been carrying her for the past twenty miles."

In other words, the act may have long been stopped and the darkness of consciousness of the perpetrator long since corrected, but if we keep holding to the memory of the wrong, it is we who are now breaking the law. This has shocking implications for every person who is carrying the burden of unforgiveness over personal wrongs committed and even over the collective wrongs such as the Jews' feelings about the crimes of the Nazis. It is not difficult to identify with the feelings of persons like Wiesenthal, for what greater crime has been committed in all history than that done to the Jews under Nazi Germany. But when we know the law, we should also be saddened to know that in persons like Wiesenthal there is such a continued frustration of love. Love is the only way the true problem can ever be resolved. Their hurt is understandable and their sincerity and commitment unquestionable. Yet these persons may be creating a further human nurture of bands of hate and the frustration of love.

We talk of forgiveness as if it were something we can easily do by an act of will. As love is not the plaything of human volition but the action of divine law, so forgiveness is not achieved by simply saying, "All right, I am going to forgive this thing." We might be saying it through clenched fists and gritted teeth, adding, "I will—if it kills me!" To forgive means to pass from judgment to understanding. It is turning from dealing with life at the surface with its differences and slights and injustices between people, to going deep down into the well of spiritual insight, touching the underground stream of love where we can know, with Emerson, that I am my brother and my brother is me. Thus we forgive ourselves for judging our brother which was thus a judgment of ourself. We turn from resistance and resentment to love, letting it heal the hurt and bind up the broken circuitry of our life.

We have rationalized our willful refusal to let go of unforgiveness with the concept of the "unforgivable sin." Nothing is unforgivable by law —the law of Divine Love. Theologically, the "unforgivable sin" is simply the closed mind. God can do no more for man than He can do through man. If the mind of man is made up in prejudice and bitterness, then the love of God cannot do its healing work. If we insist upon carrying our hurt and our guilt, then we must go on punishing ourselves; but it is self-punishment for our refusal to forgive ourselves.

It is sad how many religious practices rationalize the evils of the world as being under divine condemnation, thus condoning and even encouraging human judgment and unforgiveness. Yet Jesus said, "If you are offering your gift at the altar, and there remember that your brother has something against you, leave your gift there before the altar and go; first be reconciled to your brother, and then come and offer your gift" (Matt. 5:23, 24). Why? Because prayer that is closed to the forgiveness of transcendental love is a mockery. Prayer, as Emerson puts it, is "the contemplation of the facts of life from the highest point of view."[3] The highest point of view is the insight of the pure in heart which sees God. True prayer must be based on "In the beginning . . . love," and its end must be letting go of wrongdoing and the memory of wrong, rising to the consciousness of the omnipresence of God and the Allness of love.

Someone has said, "When you are sick of being sick, you will get well." Back of this is the realization that health is natural, and sickness is caused and perpetuated by an unnatural influence of negative thoughts and emotions. It is equally true that when you are tired of bitterness and hatred and the steel bands of unforgiveness, you will let go of the whole involvement with the ego, and without further effort on your part love and forgiveness will "spring forth speedily."

When you stop dealing with things at the level of the human and begin letting the divine of you express through the transcendence of love which has always been the reality of you, suddenly you will have the whole universe on your side. When mankind as a whole decides that it is fed up with walls of separation and the wars that result, the walls will come down. Men and women will begin to emphasize likenesses instead of differences. People will build bridges instead of complaining about the gaps in understanding or credibility, and turn on lights instead of cursing the darkness.

Of course, if you realize that you are a creature of love, created in the image-likeness of God who is love, that love is always the reality of you at the depth of you, and that *life is for loving*, then forgiveness is academic in your life, for you will not judge persons or take offense at their actions. However, if you find yourself feeling the "slings and arrows of outrageous fortune" and especially centering your attention upon the evil acts of certain persons, it might be wise to search your own mind and heart. Perhaps you have turned off your light of love, or you may be frustrating the Allness of love in you through preoccupation with the sinful world "out there." Forgive yourself for trying to find in the world that which can only be found within yourself.

Jesus said, "In the world you have tribulation; but be of good cheer, I have overcome the world" (John 16:33). The overcoming power is now as it has always been the creative power of transcendental love. You are created in and of this love. And you always have enough love within you to solve every problem. You need only to let go and "let God *be* God in you," and to let Love *be* love in you—let Love BE you. For *life is for loving*.

3. *From Loneliness to Oneness*

The study of love must rightly begin with some theory of human existence. All of us at some time in the past were born. And in the process of birth we experienced a tremendous shock—emerging from the security and warmth of the womb into a world of insecurity and a future that was indefinite and unknown. Out from an experience of complete oneness we were cut off to become fearfully aware of separation. We became desperately dependent on others and on the cooperation of outer forces that did not always cooperate.

Thus, all through our lives, one of our deepest needs is to overcome our separateness, to leave the prison of aloneness. It could be said that the absolute failure to achieve this aim means insanity because the panic of complete isolation can be overcome only by such a radical withdrawal from the world outside. In this state, the feeling of separation disappears because the world outside, from which we are separated, has disappeared.

Thomas Wolfe has captured this whole experience in *Look Homeward Angel*, when he says: "Naked and alone we came into exile. In her dark womb we did not know our mother's face, from the prison of her flesh have we come into the unspeakable and incommunicable prison of this earth. Which of us has known his brother? Which of us has looked into his father's heart? Which of us has not remained forever prison-pent? Which of us is not forever a stranger and alone . . . lost! Remembering speechlessly we seek the great forgotten language, the lost lane-end into heaven: An unfound door. Where? When?"[1]

The feeling of loneliness is one of the greatest challenges of human experience. And the strange thing is: It has little to do with the proximity of other persons. We need only to wander through the streets of a large city and note the sadness and fear and isolation of large masses of people who are even being jostled about by one another to see the aptness of the descriptive phrase, "the lonely crowd." On the other hand we may sit beside a mountain lake, companioned only by the whisper of the wind through the sturdy pine trees and the trickle of water in the friendly brook, and be secure and at one, though the nearest neighbor is two miles down a seldom traveled road.

What is loneliness? Obviously, it is not the same thing as being alone. Loneliness is completely psychological; a deficiency of spirit. And it can only be corrected by overcoming that deficiency.

Many things may conspire to create a situation in which we are alone: living alone, meeting the changes and challenges of life alone, living our life essentially on our own. It is true that such situations usually result in a terrible, even chronic, state of loneliness for the individual. But it need not be so.

"Poor lonely Fred" is the object of much sympathy by those who work with him. He is an efficient and cooperative worker, pleasant and well-mannered, but with a constant air of sadness about him. In the evening, as his co-workers return expectantly and joyously to their lives of involvement, Fred always seems to linger reluctantly at his desk and then ultimately depart from the office almost in dread of going off into darkness of a friendless world and home to his lonely apartment.

One night the office staff arranged a party for "poor Fred." They thought of all the things that should help him to feel wanted and loved, even introducing him to a woman who they thought might make a lovely companion for him. Their intentions were good. They really thought that if Fred were surrounded for a few hours by happy people that it would "cheer him up." But the results were disastrous. Oh, all the guests had a wonderful time. But the purpose of the gathering was to help Fred to escape his loneliness, but, in fact, he sat most of the evening in the farthest corner he could find, alone, and lonely.

The fact is, Fred is not an unfortunate person who has been separated from life by circumstances over which he has no control. He is lonely, not because he hasn't discovered the right friends, but because he has not discovered himself. He has not discovered his oneness with the Infinite Power and Presence of God within him by which he may build the only possible bridge with the world around him. He may complain that he has no friends, and no opportunity to make them. But he usually arranges things in this way so that he will not be faced with the need to put up barriers to prevent people from getting close to him.

Fred is really lonely because he is alienated from his real self, the self of him that is created in the image-likeness of God who is love. He thinks that the absence of love in his life is due both to the fact that his parents did not display love to him, and by some quirk of fate people have always seemed to treat him in this same unfriendly and loveless way all his life. But his problem is that he has strayed in consciousness into the "far country," away from the reality of his being which is always centered in love. His loneliness is not the result of conditions; for conditions may be anything from crowds to isolation. His loneliness is, rather, a conditioned reflex in which he habitually reacts to *all* conditions.

What Fred's associates did not know is that loneliness cannot be overcome by getting something. His life could only be changed by a change of consciousness within himself. The love he needs is within himself. He must give. His problem is not that people have been withholding from him, but that he has been frustrating his potential of transcendental love, withholding it from those about him.

Perhaps you can identify with "poor Fred." There may be a little of "Fred" in all of us. The need is to "unlearn our errors." You are a creature of love, created in the image and likeness of God who is love. Love is your very nature. Like Fred, you are lonely, not because you have no one to love you or because people in general are not loving to you. You are lonely because you are frustrating the one source of love within you and are hopelessly looking for love and acceptance from others. Without the acceptance of love within you, you are unable to accept love from others even when it is sincerely proffered. For until you touch the love that is you, you can never touch the love that is another.

The only way you can overcome the feeling of loneliness and separation is by realizing the continuity of God's love for you: "I have loved thee with an everlasting love." Turn your thoughts within and feel the warmth and support of this eternal fountain of love in which you live and have being. You are *in* love; no matter what the conditions of your environment. You can then look about you in friendliness, knowing for all persons, "I am *in* love with you. We are *in* love together."

Obviously this takes wise and careful thought so that you do not become vulnerable to deceptive fantasies in yourself and to the destructive intent of others. If you prepare yourself through deep and intensive meditation upon the reality of your own oneness in the Allness of love, this will be a guiding and protecting presence to you in all your ways. Then you can practice the presence of love, knowing for everyone you meet—people on the street, in the subway or bus, in your office or shop or apartment building: "I am *in* love with you; we are *in* love together." This will not only give you a warm feeling of unity that will dissolve all loneliness, but it is also the most effective shield from any kind of harm. "He that dwelleth in the secret place of the Most High, shall abide under the shadow of the Almighty" (Ps. 91:1, ASV).

Dane Rudhyar, author of many books on astrology, says that Jesus gave us an antidote to the sickness of isolation in self. He calls it "mutuality," which means interchange or the "one another" in all that we do. He points out that the first great test of the spiritual life is isolation. All important things begin in isolation, but they mature through mutuality. While selfhood is singleness; love is cooperative sharing. So he says that what begins in self must understand and realize itself in "mutuality and in love."

One of the deepest mysteries of life is that every individual in the world stands alone; he lives his life alone and can never really be united with anyone in a purely physical sense. Each person lives in a separate world, the world of his own thinking. Just as no two atoms ever really touch each other even in the most compact of substances, so no two individuals ever completely touch each other, even in the most beautiful relationship of husband and wife. There are always some reserves, some barriers, something withheld. It is only through the highest form of love that these barriers are occasionally dissolved. And this is right, for each is an individual, and individuality must not be smothered by possessiveness. As Gibran so beautifully phrases it, "Let there be spaces in your togetherness."[2]

The person who is possessive, oversolicitous, and overprotective of a husband or wife, of children, or of friends is essentially jealous because he is afraid of being lonely. He desperately holds on to people, telling them and deluding himself that it is his desire to care for and protect them due to his great love for them. He believes that love is the projection of his own ego, thus it is limited. He doesn't know that inner-centered love has no end. Actually, his concern for the well-being of his loved ones is a fear of losing them. Not that he loves them so much, but that he wants them for his own, because they are his shield from himself, from his gnawing desert of loneliness within himself.

There can be no jealousy in love. In the oneness which love reveals, there are security and freedom. The wise person will interpret signs of jealousy or possessiveness in himself as an evidence that he has moved from his own center in love. He will know that it means, not that he loves so very much, but that he loves too little in the reality of inner-centered love. Instead of being motivated by suspicion and distrust, he will spend time in quiet meditation, "calling to remembrance" his own true being that is centered in the love that is God. In this consciousness he can bless his loved one with the realization that "we are *in* love together."

In the heart of every person there is an awful homesickness for God, for wholeness, for relatedness, for unity. It comes from an intuitive awareness of the reality of his true being *in* love. It is this homesickness for God, for inner oneness, that, misinterpreted, leads to the frantic search for friends and the indulgence of self in things. St. Augustine obviously knew this, for in the very beginning of his *Confessions* he prays, "Thou hast formed us for Thyself, and our hearts are restless till they find rest in Thee."[3] It is the part longing for the whole, the human self longing for unity with the Universal Self. And this unity is what love really is.

Each self is not only unique in itself, but it is also a unique individualization of the whole, of God. In our deeper being, all beings are One Being, and all individual selves are One Self. Thus, when we realize our unity with God, we feel a flow of love, and a sense of oneness with all persons. It is like going down into a well within ourselves and coming to a deep underground stream, immersing ourselves in that stream and then discovering that the same stream is within every person and at the heart of him he too is immersed in it with us. This is what is meant by being *in* love with all persons. This oneness is love in action.

Lack of this awareness of spiritual unity, the oneness of all life, of all persons, leads to inner loneliness which has often been called "social anemia." It also leads to all forms of selfishness; envy, anger, and hate; all pride, vanity, conceit, contempt for others; all injustice, greed, cruelty, and crime; all beliefs in the superiority of oneself and the inferiority of others—hence the so-called "race problem." We can see, thus, that most of the problems of society, or of "man's inhumanity to man," are the result of the failure of persons to know themselves as creatures of love, centered in the love that is God. The great illusion that men are private, separate selves, living private, separate lives, having private, separate existences, with private, separate fates and destinies, has created all the disunity in the world since time began. Thus, it is true, "What the world needs is love," an awareness on the part of people that they are created in the image and likeness of God who is love. In the consciousness of this innateness of love, there can be only love and good will for all other persons, no matter who or what or where they are.

Civilization has arisen completely on the emergence of love within man, and the future of mankind can be made sure only by the renewed commitment of "men of good will" to the practice of the presence of love in all personal and international relations. We must condition ourselves to look with eyes of love at our fellow creatures, to look beneath the surface and recognize the true Self in one another, rather than reacting negatively to the surface selves with which we are constantly coming into conflict.

Loneliness may at times be related to our conditioning to the idea of being "socially accepted." In this consciousness we need always to prove that we are a "social success" by being sought after and by never being alone. If one is well-liked, that is, socially successful (or so the idea goes), one will rarely be alone. Willie Loman, in Arthur Miller's *Death of a Salesman*, advises his sons, "Be well-liked, and you will never want."[4] And yet Willie was the very epitome of the bleak and lonely existence.

The greatest tragedy for many persons is the feeling of being "on the outside," the sense of being alienated from the crowd. This leads to a compulsive worship of everything that is "in"—wearing certain style clothes, reading certain books, seeing certain plays, even showing an interest in new trends in religion, or psychology, or politics. "It is the 'in' thing to do!"

Or—it may be expressed in terms of the importance of being invited to "this party" or "that dinner." Not because we have any vital interest in it, but because being invited is proof that we are not left out, that we are socially acceptable. And we can see this same motivation behind the compulsion to get into certain fields of work, and the pressure for promotions to certain levels within a field. The paradox is: The person goes into a field because he fears the loneliness of being left out, and then he faces the awesome loneliness of living out his life in a work totally divorced from the natural inclination and talent of his own uniqueness.

Loneliness is a painful threat to many who have no conception of the positive value of solitude. They will often settle for the cheapest and even the most sordid kind of preoccupation or entertainment as an escape from the bleakness of being alone. André Gide says that most people suffer from the fear of finding themselves alone and so they don't find themselves at all.

The average person is reactive in thought and experience. He reacts to suggestions, he reacts to what happens in the world, he reacts to people in conversation—leading to "small talk." His whole thought process is reactive in nature. He engages in little or no introspection or original thinking. Thus, when this person is alone, he has little if anything to react to, and his security is threatened, for life has lost its continuity, and therefore its meaning. Of course, it was never really a meaning—only an illusion; but the sense of loneliness is oppressive.

This is not true with the creative person, the original thinker. He is not at all disturbed by being alone. Actually he is enthusiastic about the prospect, for he will thus be free from the distractions of people and events and will be able to engage in serious thought and creativity.

Man is never less alone than when he is alone. A mystic teacher who had lived alone in a cave in the high mountains of Himalaya was being interviewed by a reporter. He was asked, "But aren't you terribly lonely out here by yourself?" The beautifully composed holy man replied, "I wasn't lonely until you came!" This is a concept that is difficult for the Western mind to grasp, for it reflects the commitment to solitude as a way of life.

Man's great poverty is in his loss of the sense of innateness, and of the importance of going apart from time to time to cultivate it. It is the sense of unity, of wholeness, of being *in* love, that is the basis of solitude. In our day we have a false sense that life must be all busyness. Life must be go-go-go, do-do-do. Even recreation and vacations become pressure-laden with a competitive spirit and pressure-packed itineraries. We feel that there is no time for solitude or meditation, when our state of mind and body may indicate that it should be given the first priority.

We tend to cripple our children, for we do not realize their need for solitude. We try to make them happy by keeping them entertained and involved. Thus the child grows up with the idea that life is a constant effort to escape boredom. The cry of the adolescent is, "What do they do for excitement around here?" In time they join the adult society on the treadmill of involvement to escape the awful sense of loneliness that each carries with him wherever he goes. It becomes a sickness whose only cure is in the rediscovery of the deeper self that is created in the image-likeness of God who is love.

Strange are the foibles of our Western culture. It is permissible to say that you are lonely, for most people are—and it is a way of admitting that it is not good to be alone. And—it is permissible to want to be alone temporarily, to "get away from it all." But—if one indicates that he enjoys being alone, not for rest or escape, but for its own joys, people think that there is something vaguely wrong with him.

Anne Lindbergh comments on this in her delightful book, *Gift from the Sea:* "The world today does not understand, in either man or woman, the need to be alone. . . . Anything else will be accepted as a better excuse. If one sets aside time for a business appointment, that time is accepted as inviolable. But if one says: I cannot come because that is my hour to be alone, one is considered rude, egotistical, or strange. What a commentary on our civilization, when being alone is considered suspect; when one has to apologize for it, make excuses, hide the fact that one practices it—like some 'secret vice.' "[5]

Recall that we all started out in this life being propelled into a prison of aloneness, and that we have a deep need to escape, to overcome the sense of separateness. Misreading the true need, we seek to escape our aloneness by involvement "out there" in the world of people and things and changing experiences. We are centered in love within ourselves, but we have lost our consciousness of the center. The need is not to escape into the world, but to escape *to* the center, to find our oneness with God in the reality of our wholeness in love. Any attempt to relate in the world without this consciousness of who and what we are will result in problems which often lead to a retreat into a complex of fear and loneliness.

Thus, the cure for loneliness, strange as it may seem, is not in more active involvement in the world, but in seeking active unfoldment from within of our essential self which has been isolated. The lonely person needs to cultivate the art of creative solitude, to plumb the depths of his inmost self through meditation, to get away from people and relationships and become established in the root of reality in God—in love. Loneliness is not a longing for people but for God. Thus, the answer is not in the bingo parlor or friendship club or in social busyness. It is in self-discovery and self-realization. It is in reflecting upon God *as* love, knowing that you are "loved with an everlasting love," and that you are always *in* love. You can never be alone!

Take time to practice the presence of God, the activity of love. Know that you are *in* love wherever you are, and that love is *in* you as an attracting, healing, harmonizing, and totally fulfilling power. Let your awareness of love begin to transcend the exclusiveness of loving one person, and thus to heal the hurt that may persist over the loss or absence of that one person. An excellent basis for this kind of contemplation would be some thoughts such as these from Erich Fromm's *Art of Loving:*

Love is not primarily a relationship to a specific person; it is an attitude, an orientation of character which determines the relatedness of a person to the world as a whole, not toward one "object" of love. If a person loves only one other person and is indifferent to the rest of his fellow man, his love is not love but a symbiotic attachment, or an enlarged egotism. Yet most people believe that love is constituted by the object and not by the faculty. Because one does not see that love is an activity, a power of the soul, one believes that all that is necessary to find is the right object—and that everything goes by itself afterward. This attitude can be compared to that of a man who wants to paint but who, instead of learning the art, claims that he has just to wait for the right object, and that he will paint beautifully when he finds it. If I truly love one person, I love all persons, I love the world, I love life. If I can say to somebody else, "I love you," I must be able to say, "I love you in everybody, I love through you the world, I love in you also myself."[6]

You can grow from loneliness to oneness, but it will take effort. You will need to realize the reality of love that is always present, and you will have to practice its presence. You may feel that your loneliness will give way to oneness when your "true love" comes along. Don't delude yourself! It is not in finding the right person, but in being the right person that leads to the fulfillment in love. Love is an energy force with fantastic possibilities for your life; but it is not to be found in human relations —only in the depth of your inmost self. When you find and experience it at the depth of you, your whole consciousness will be centered in love. Without conscious effort you will love things, love the world, love flowers and trees and people on the street. You will easily become a channel for unrestricted love to flow through, and an instrument for the creative process of the Infinite to do its wonderful work under the warming, healing, and prospering influence of that love.

You will feel loved and secure and protected wherever you may be. And you will have solved the problem of loneliness forever. You will never be afraid of being alone again, nor will you ever again be lonely when you are alone. And—you will become amazingly attractive and socially acceptable. You will be invited everywhere, with friends and loving companionship beyond the point imaginable. But most important, if it is your desire, into this dynamic flow of happy and fulfilling relationships will come one person with whom you can become mutually beloved. For, as it is written, "It is not good that man [or woman] should be alone" (Gen. 2:18).

4. *What God Hath Joined*

Among the changing values and institutions of modern times, none has been of any greater concern to the "viewers with alarm" than the rapid erosion of the institution of marriage; not only through divorce, but through newly emerging life-styles. Since the family has always been the backbone of our culture, there is every reason to examine carefully the changing patterns, and to ask some frank, honest, and possibly painful questions.

A recent magazine reported a study detailing some of the changing mores of marriage; citing some 2,158,000 marriage licenses issued in 1972 and 773,000 divorces granted. It talked about the changing traditions of marriage by reason of the demands people are making for new quality in marriage, the search for new kinds of honest human relationships that so much of our synthetic culture denies them. It dealt with such things as "group marriage," living together unmarried, "marriage contracts," and with the hypocrisy involved in many "stable marriages."

A woman recently said, "I have come to the conclusion that the problem with most marriages is inflated expectations. After a brief period of abnormal ecstasy, it is inevitable that the relationship will settle into a humdrum existence of 'quiet desperation.' There are no truly happy marriages. There are only people who have the ability to make the best of things, whatever they are." But even as she said all of this, there was a wistful look in her eyes that said, "I wish this were not the case!"

Are there no happy marriages? Or is it really true that a marriage, like a job, is what the person makes it? People often look enviously at those who have "interesting" jobs. But there are no interesting jobs. There are only interested people who invest a very special spark and spirit in everything they do, lending an aura of enchantment to their involvement, which, incidentally, may well be the secret of success. Is marriage, then, simply an attitude in the minds of people? Does a marriage ever succeed—or fail? Or is it people who succeed or fail in giving themselves wholly to each other? Or, on the other hand, isn't there more to marriage than two people getting along? There is the question of the *two people;* who they are, what drew them together, and what is the "tie that binds."

And then there is the inescapable fact of divorce. Why do divorces occur? Is divorce wrong? Should people stay together "till death do us part"? Actually the percentages of divorces do not really tell the full story of the breakdown of the institution of marriage—for millions of marriages remain intact institutionally where they are totally divided spiritually and in love. Is divorce immoral or is it more immoral to continue in a marriage that is spiritually broken?

What and why is marriage? A little boy once asked the question of his grandmother. She said, "When two people love each other and decide they can get along with each other forever, they get married." This satisfied the young fellow and he thoughtfully walked away. Sometime later the wise grandmother heard the boy and his playmates noisily playing "cops and robbers" under her window. "Bang, bang, you're dead! Bang, bang, you're dead!" Suddenly the voice of her grandson called out, "Aw, come on! Let's don't kill each other; let's get married!"

"Let's get married!" Common to all persons through all time has been the restless yearning for union, for wholeness. Perhaps it is beyond explanation, but it is this basic urge that leads men and women to seek companionship and love. Some would say that the basic drive is the production of offspring by the union of the sexes, but there is a deeper motivation and a much broader implication. Certainly the urge for mating and parenthood is basic to the human species. There is also the fact that marriage is given the hallmark of social approval, and that "old maids" and bachelors are never really accepted as socially adjusted persons.

Deep within every person there is a vision of love and wholeness, an intuitive sense of his own oneness with God, and with his fellow man —and the yearning for a special kind of oneness with a very special kind of person who will bring wholeness to his life. It is undoubtedly the yearning for this ideal state that will not permit him to settle for anything less or to be satisfied with the "arrangement," the marriage that is legally and sacramentally consummated, even though it is spiritually sterile.

One of the basic problems of marriage and of the ensuing incidence of divorce is that people are led into marriage for many reasons other than true love. The startling thing is that the pressures are so great that the person is not even aware of the absence of true love. Marriage is entered into for convenience, for economic necessity, for common interests, for sexual fulfillment, and under the pressures of society's mores: "At your age you should be married; what's wrong with you?" Lonely people often think more of finding someone who will marry them than of finding the attraction of a true mate. Perhaps the greatest miracle is that as many marriages work out as do under the circumstances.

The one great problem in marriage is the lack of insight into this thing called love. Love is a relatively rare phenomenon in our society, despite the fact that there are many relationships and emotions that are called "love." It is a word that is almost totally abused and perverted in that it is often used as a repository for insincerity and hypocrisy.

We have been conditioned to an exterior-orientation of life. "Out here is where it's at," says the existentialist. Thus love is something you find and then something you "make." Love is an object, then, instead of a faculty. The emphasis is placed upon ways of attracting and appealing to the object of love. In our culture what most persons mean by being lovable, is being popular and having sex appeal. Marriages that come about in this way are rarely successful. There may be an attraction of bodies, but no innate sense of union. What is left but to settle into the "arrangement"?

Persons in this "arrangement" go through the motions, playing the role of lovers and friends; but if there is no feeling of oneness within and between them, there is little release of transcendental love. Even if there is an understanding of the importance of saying loving words and doing loving acts, it is only a constant *attempt* to be loving. However, love is not trying; it is being. To try to be loving is to be totally barren of the kind of love that is imperative for a healthy marriage.

Love is a divine attribute of man who is fundamentally a spiritual being. To talk about love and leave out God is like talking about making hay while the sun shines and omit the sun. God is what love is all about, and love is what God is all about. And the one is as undefinable as the other. Love can be understood only in the context of the whole person. Love is not an emotion, love is not sensual, love is not sex; though it may and should use these areas of experience as a conduit through which it naturally flows in the process of communion. But the communion is, or should be, a transcendent thing.

To understand marriage, the union of two persons, we need to understand that every person has a changeless and eternal spiritual union with God. This is not something to be earned or created; it is the reality of the true being of every person. The yearning for love and the communion with another person is basically the yearning to know and be the whole person that we essentially are. This is why Eckhart sees the transcendent goal of life as to "let God be God in you." "God created man in his own image." And God is love. Therefore we are created in and of love. We are creatures of love with an inexhaustible potential of love within us. The yearning for love is the sense of "oughtness" based on the intuitive sense of ISness. We yearn to "let love be love in us."

The dream of love seems to be an "impossible dream" simply because we try to achieve in the outer that which can only be found within. We think we can "fall in love" with one person, but actually we are "*in* love" with all persons, for all persons are created in and of love. The falling in love might better be described as falling *from* love, falling from an "inner-centered" love to the "outer-centered" experience of indulging the emotions and the sexual feelings. This is the great human crisis that can be most misleading. It is the easiest thing in the world for two lonely persons to fall in love, and then to assume that they are meant for each other. The important criterion, which may well be the missing link of marriage, is: Can they *rise in love* beyond the attraction of bodies to the transcendent sense of spiritual union?

What we are saying here is that being in love with someone is not a sufficient basis for marriage, simply because in the Cosmic scheme of things all persons are *in* love with all persons. Love most certainly is the basis of all relationships, and there is a very special experience of love in the most perfect relationship of man and woman in marriage. But there is something more.

It has been said, almost as a cliché, "Marriages are made in heaven." And it is true, though not in the way this statement is usually interpreted. The true marriage comes about because of transcendent and not human forces; not as a result of sex appeal or material means, but two people being drawn together by "an irresistible attraction" and sensing and seeing in each other something of the divine potential that is always present beyond appearances. This may lead to a mutual commitment to help each other mate with one's God-self. It is this consciousness and vision of the true "helpmate" that is the basis of the perfect marriage. It can happen only between persons who are transcendentally and not just physically attracted. It reflects a love that is without ego, without the motivation of self-fulfillment or sense desire. The fulfillment of self and satisfaction of the senses may follow, and should do so. But if they come first there can never be more than an "arrangement" without depth.

When two persons "fall in love" there follows a sense involvement and an "ego trip." At this point love is not only blind, it is selfish. The partners are vulnerable to hurt for they are insecure in their consciousness of the innateness of love. How can they know if their relationship is or can be on the level of the spiritual "helpmate"? They will know by whether or not they can truly let go of self and its wants and urges. The law is: The integrity of the person is inviolable. To use another person is to violate that person's rights as an individual, making an object of him or her; and in violating the integrity of another you actually violate your own. Out of this comes a subtle resentment that progressively erodes the only basis the relationship had—the using of another for the fulfillment of self.

In all enjoyment there is a choice between enjoying the other and enjoying oneself through the instrumentality of the other. The first is the enjoyment of love, the second is the enjoyment of lust. The first is the basis for the "helpmate," the second is totally inadequate as a basis for any enduring relationship. When persons enjoy themselves through each other, they do not really meet as persons—their reality is lost. They meet as the ghosts of themselves, and thus their pleasure is a ghostly pleasure that cannot begin to satisfy the human soul, which thus corrupts its capacity for reality.

Jesus had a very high vision of the love that finds fulfillment in marriage: "Have you not read that he who made them from the beginning made them male and female, and said, 'For this reason a man shall leave his father and mother and be joined to his wife, and the two shall become one'? So they are no longer two but one. What God has joined together, let no man put asunder" (Matt. 19:4–6).

This seems clear enough—and certainly it does appear unequivocally to prohibit divorce. But what hath God joined? Can union be brought about by a priestly "I pronounce thee . . ." if there is no union within? If God joins something together, can it be put asunder? Man is relentlessly held to the earth by gravity. Can this "joining" be put asunder? God is law—not caprice. The law might better be stated, "What God joins together, no man can put asunder."

Spiritual union is not a bequest but a conquest. First, it is the conquest of self; the sense-indulgent desires, the possessive urges, the ego-centered ideals. It has been said that all marriages must begin with divorce —the divorce of each person from self. The words "I love you" more often than not mean "I love me and I want you for myself." This is essentially what the "falling in love" consciousness means. Unless there is a willingness to rise out of this indulgence of self into the selfless attitude of the helpmate, true spiritual union is not possible.

Goethe says that marriage is an opportunity to grow. The achievement of the spiritual union may require years of growth in the process of mating the self to the Spirit between two persons and within each one. It requires a continued commitment, and yet unless it is a commitment that comes easily and naturally, there is evidence of a lack of "rightness." For even as to try to be loving reflects an absence of love, so also to try to be committed indicates that there is no basis to make the commitment real.

When two persons are committed to being a helpmate to each other, there is a progressive growth, both individually and in the depth of the relationship. There is an experience of deep and fulfilling transcendent love, which makes all things right. In this relationship there may be obstacles but none are insurmountable. There is simply a continuous adventure of growth, accompanied by an increasing appreciation for each other.

In a healthy, mutually supportive marriage relationship "no man can put it asunder." There is no jealousy or fear, for there is a strong consciousness of oneness that cannot be disturbed. As Gibran suggests, there is a willingness to have "spaces in the togetherness." Some states have laws allowing damages for "alienation of affections." But love is not a commodity that can be bought, sold, traded, or stolen. When a lover or spouse is "stolen" by another person, that person was already ripe for the stealing. He was already predisposed toward a new relationship. The "love bandit" was only taking what was waiting to be taken, what wanted to be taken. The "third party" merely served as a pretext for dissolving a marriage that was the façade for an empty lie.

Now, if spiritual union is not a bequest, but a conquest, possibly requiring years of growth, isn't it possible that the union may never be consummated in growth, even though it is formalized legally and sacramentally? And, since life is growth, isn't it also possible that the pace and direction of growth may vary, and that the two might conceivably grow apart instead of together? Religious tradition has not allowed for this possibility, but has been closed-minded about situations in which it is self-evident. "Till death do us part" has been the rigid commandment. People in a deteriorating marriage have had no other recourse than to continue with the "arrangement," gritting their teeth in an attitude of "We'll make it work if it kills us." The sad part is that psychologically and even physically, it often does just that. There is a growing awareness that many of the ills to which the flesh seems heir are actually induced by the emotions arising out of relationships that have stopped being mutually supportive and thus have become mutually destructive.

When a psychological or spiritual separation is consummated in divorce we often ask, "But what happened?" Is it not realistic to say, "Life happened!" Need we think of divorce as necessarily negative or immoral? May it not be far less moral and certainly much more destructive for such persons to remain together, living a lie that deceives few persons? It certainly does not deceive the offspring they may delusively remain together for the sake of.

In physics the force of gravity also involves a kind of anti-gravity, and the attraction of bodies when reversed becomes repulsion. It is the same force being dealt with in different ways. The force is constant, the experience of it changes. In the unity of all life, man is forever being drawn toward oneness or wholeness. In his changing consciousness this may draw him *to* relationships, experiences, jobs, etc.; or it may lead him *from* them to a new demonstration of his unfolding good. Some persons willfully hold on, saying, "But this is my right place!" One of the great lessons of life is that the "right place" is not a static experience, but a state of consciousness.

The great goal of life is spiritual union—the oneness of the human and the divine within the individual. In a true marriage there is a mutual attraction of a helpmate into the lives of two persons. This helpmate is one who has the commitment to help the beloved to mate with his or her true Self. If the marriage is to be successful it must serve to bring the partners closer to their Christ selves. If it appears to fail it serves (or should do so) to lead them on to new experiences that can facilitate the progression from self to Spirit. There is no real failure in marriage, or in any experience in life, other than the failure to respond to the obvious signals of the Spirit to "walk on!" The great majority of marriage failures are those in which the partners are trying to hide the fact that they are living a lie, living out an "arrangement" in which there is no consciousness of the "helpmate" and no presence of transcendental love.

Life is a continuous process of growth through change. "What God hath joined together" refers to the changeless relationship each person has with Spirit, with Infinite Mind, and with the principle of "I have loved thee with an everlasting love." But all else in consciousness and in life is changing and *must* change. Man should always seek to find the growth experience in every situation and relationship. But if it ceases to be mutually supportive and becomes instead mutually destructive, then divorce may be strongly indicated as a constructive step toward union and wholeness. Society must realistically face up to the place of divorce as a part of the growth experience in marriage. Not as a means of escape from the pain of growth, but as a recognition that, as Gibran puts it, "your pain is the breaking of the shell that encloses your understanding."[1] At times the growth potential of the individuals can be fulfilled only by the breaking of the bond that ties, painful as that breakup might be.

But, of course, the important thing is not how to get out of marriage, but how to understand the ISness of love, how to become true "helpmates," and how to establish true spiritual unity—both as preparations for marriage, and as growth experiences within it. Marriage, in the ideal, is the finest possible workshop for personal development, replete with the growth opportunities of "getting along"; but also with the marvelous provision of the helpmate who through the dedication of selfless love helps his or her beloved to achieve wholeness as a person through the progressive mating of the self to the Spirit.

5. Love and Sex

A few years ago Murray Schisgal did a play on Broadway entitled *LUV*. In the preface to the play he says, "The sense of it [the title] is that the emotion of love has been perverted and misused to such an extent that it can be defined only by using another word which comes closer to what we experience, to what we think and how we behave. It can be l-u-v, l-o-v, or x-y-z, but it certainly can't be a word that has been abused as much as l-o-v-e. L-u-v is the perversion of love. I don't have the audacity to define the other."[1]

Perhaps no other word in the Western world has been so abused as "love"—in our literature as well as in our lives, and at all levels, from the romantic to the religious to the parental. A good example of this is found in the antiwar slogan of the counterculture of today's young people: "Make Love and Not War!" Of itself, this is a great idea; but when the slogan adorns a poster with the picture of a nude woman suggesting sensuality, it is a mockery.

In the first place, the term "make love" indicates an almost universal misunderstanding of what love is. A man and woman may indulge themselves in sensual appetites, but of itself this is not necessarily an expression or experience of love. Love can be understood only in the context of the whole person. To repeat: Love is *not* an emotion, love is *not* sensual, love is *not* sex—though it may and should use these elements as a conduit through which it naturally flows in the process of communion. But the communion is, or should be, a transcendent thing.

Due to the Puritan rigidity of values under which many of us have been reared, it may seem shocking that we would deal with the sexual element in human relations in what is otherwise a very spiritual treatment of the subject of love. But, how can we understand the fullness of love unless we can relate it to every aspect of the love experience? Love is not sex, and yet the fullness of love in perfect communion of man and woman may overflow into an experience of sexual stimulation and fulfillment. It is not sex that is base, but the misuse of sex in the addiction to sensual things. For how can anything that happens between people in the total experience of love be impure?

In Genesis we read, ". . . male and female created he them." And again, "It is not good for man to be alone." So, in one's search for wholeness, one seeks a very special communion with the Spirit indwelling and also with a beloved person with whom to share the adventure of unfoldment. And in the wholeness of this communion there is, and should be, a very beautiful physical relationship that needs to be understood.

Today sex is big business. It certainly would appear by all the advertising themes that we dote on it and are motivated by it. The sex theme is used more often than any other to sell bread, cigars, perfume, books, movies, and even political doctrines. As persons, we make use of sexual allure and prowess to prove our power, to demonstrate that we are acceptable, free, sophisticated, or courageous; or we repress our sexual drives to prove ourselves pure and noble. Yet not one of these things is proper to our sexual endowment, and certainly not one of them is love.

When we so dote on sex as to believe that sexual energy is the primary ground and foundation of love, we enter into a whirl of confusion that is totally inimical to love. A psychologist friend, who has caught the transcendental nature of man, flatly asserts that "there is no such thing as sex." He means that sex is not a *thing* in itself, but that it is a function of the whole person. And the sex part of a relationship takes its meaning from the total union between two people *as people*, not just as sex partners.

Man is a physical creature, with certain undeniable biological urges and sense appetites. But man is more than an animal. He is potentially a divine creature, and through love he is raised from a mere biological organism to the level of his divinity. It is love alone that can enable man to relate harmoniously with fellow creatures without feuding and war. It is only through love that man can become creative and self-disciplined and truly human. Certain it is that no marriage can endure as a place of harmony and creative living without that something through which the persons involved can transcend their animal impulses. That something is love!

It is unfortunate that sex is so often equated with love. Sex, as it is normally viewed, is the copulation or physical joining of two bodies. Love is the total communion of two whole persons. The latter may—and its fullest experience should—incorporate the former. But the former may be experienced in complete absence of the latter. He who indulges in sex without love is never satisfied. He talks of his "love life" and boasts of his "love conquests." But he goes from one experience to another, seeking in quantity that which can only be found in quality, seeking in sex that which can only be found in true love.

It is also unfortunate that sexologists often have the greatest influence on marriage partners trying to find adjustment in marriage. The ideal held up is that compatibility in sexual relations will insure the perfect marriage. This is delusive and misleading. A mutual sexual attraction is no basis for an enduring relationship between a man and woman. It is an organic thing, not personal. It is purely and simply a biological impulse drawing two physical forms together. "The marriage bed" has been held up as the center of the happy home. But if the physical sharing in that bed is all that holds the partners together, the relationship is tenuous to say the least. To paraphrase Jesus' injunction, "Marriage does not live by sex alone." It is probably true that the major incidence of divorce is to be found among those relationships that come about by and are based almost entirely upon a sex involvement.

It is suggested here that you reread the previous chapter dealing with the basis for marriage. Persons in or out of marriage who engage in "sex without love," are not only prostituting themselves, but they are also selling themselves short on the real meaning of life which can be found only in the total communion of man and woman in the fullness of inner-centered or transcendental love.

In the past generation there has been a shocking "sexual revolution," which has been shattering to the old Victorian standards and to the persons who have been restricted by them. One young woman, proud of her liberation, said recently, "But sex is a perfectly natural activity, just like eating or sleeping. Why should we treat it in any other way and surround it with mystery and taboos?" Undoubtedly she is reacting to the rigid moral code of her grandmother, who was obviously wrong. But this young woman is just as wrong in another way. For sex is not a thing in itself. It is purely a way in which a person may express himself.

If we deal with sex as purely *a thing*, then we reduce ourselves totally to the level of animals. Our relationships, then, are simply on the basis of animals seeking copulation with a mate, however temporary that might be. Short of childbearing, this kind of physical coupling entails no continuity, no real human involvement, no sense of true union.

Sydney Harris, syndicated columnist and articulate commentator on the American scene, says that the modern "cult of freedom" in sex is as unrealistic as the Victorian cult of "repression." The Victorians thought that sex should never be discussed; the moderns think that hardly anything else is worth discussion. Both are perverted views, according to Harris. It is a good thing that we are casting off many of the veils that shrouded sex in the Victorian age—the subject needed daylight let in. But it is totally mistaken to put the spotlight on it; to make it a thing in itself. Certainly we need to eliminate inhibitions that keep two persons from finding a free expression of communion through love. But through the public use of four-letter words, and through pornography and X-rated movies, an emphasis is given that is degrading and perverted to the transcendent nature of man.

To young persons contemplating marriage, and to all persons who may be seeking a fulfilling relationship by which to escape their prison of aloneness, let me say with the greatest possible emphasis: THE ONLY BASIS FOR A FULFILLING MARRIAGE OR AN ENDURING MAN-WOMAN RELATIONSHIP OF ANY KIND—IS LOVE. Love may or may not include sexual attraction. It may express itself in sexual desire. But sexual desire, of itself, is not love. Desire treats its object not as a person but as a means to its own satisfaction. Mutual desire doesn't alter this position. It means only that each of two persons is treating the other as a means of self-satisfaction. A man or a woman may want each other passionately without either loving the other.

How important it is that we understand this vital point, for without this insight it is likely that we will be tempted to "sell our soul for a mess of pottage." There is a supreme moment of ecstasy in the climax of physical union; but then, without the deep and abiding love to give continuity and support and meaning to the relationship, there is only emptiness and fatigue and aloneness. A person is never more alone or lonely than at the moment beyond the climax of an experience of sex without love. This, even though he may be locked in physical embrace with his "partner."

A man and a woman may want each other for all sorts of reasons— not necessarily sexual—and make the mutual want the basis of marriage, also without either loving the other. Mutual desire, whether sexual or not, is no basis for an enduring marriage. It is the desire to obtain possession of another person for the satisfaction of personal needs. It is daring to assert the claim over another human being: "You are mine! I want you for my own! Be mine!"

As we can see, this is the theme of most of the romantic couplets that pass for poetry on greeting cards. But it is actually immoral to think in terms of possessing another person, using him or her for selfish purposes. We normally base immorality on the question of whether two people living together happen to be married. However, there may be more immorality when marriage simply covers an obvious possessiveness and indulgence of selfish and/or sensual urges. Actually, when the relationship is based on this "you are mine" attitude, there is an inroad on the integrity of a fellow human being. And the fact that the desire and claim are mutual ("We belong to each other") makes no difference.

True love, mutually shared, is the only basis on which marriage can succeed as a viable relationship. Relationships that drag on out of obligation or fear or custom are a mockery to the idea of marriage—and are actually immoral. Without this oneness of true love, it could be said that the marriage is broken before it begins, simply because the persons have broken a law which could be stated, "Whom God would keep apart, let not man put together."

It is as if a great magnet had a little battery that sent occasional magnetic charges through its poles. Iron filings could be attracted to the magnet by this temporary force. But the magnet, if it is a true magnet, has its own innate charge of energy which is constant in its attraction. The iron filings will be drawn to the poles and will remain in the magnetic field, even though they could be temporarily under the influence of the small battery charge, acting as a booster. Without the more permanent magnetic force, the filings would most certainly be scattered in disarray between the occasional surges of added attraction.

We talk about permissiveness in our society, but actually it may be that the American culture is less permissive than most others. How can we say that? Because we tend to demand, on penalty of rejection, that persons who are not really ready for a permanent relationship settle into a façade of marriage. In our country marriage is considered the norm for everyone. People who live together should be married! People who live alone at the marriageable age are odd because they don't find someone to marry! Theater people are criticized for marriages and divorces and for the complications of children from their broken homes. It could be said that these unfortunate persons were influenced to "make a mockery of marriage" because our social attitude forces them into a hypocritical conformity. Their "sex fling" is often dignified by marriage, even though by neither intention or temperament is it a permanent alliance. Inevitably the marriage is dissolved and the children are scattered to boarding schools. It might be kinder and more honest if they would simply settle for the kind of life they want to lead. They would not make a farce out of marriage, because they would not enter it. There would be no children, so there would be no violations of the obligations of parenthood. The same principle may also hold true for the average couple.

All this may evoke from the reader a reaction of shock and revulsion. Are we recommending sex without love, and life relationships without marriage? Not at all. On the contrary, let it be made very plain that any sort of union without true love by which it can become communion is but a partial experience of what life can be and should be. However, for those who "see in part" it may be the best their consciousness can achieve. It is to be hoped that they will eventually "put away childish things" and reach for a higher level of relationship.

What we are saying is that such a union is not of itself evil or immoral. It is only such when viewed from a rigid Puritanical standard—a standard which may have hurt far more lives than it has helped. But even if we insist that it is immoral for two people to live together out of wedlock, may it not be less moral for them to live together for sex or out of obligation to the children or by reason of society's taboo on divorce? In whatever way we view morality, is it not moral to be honest and immoral to lie? If two people are honest with themselves in that they do not want the responsibilities of legal marriage, should they be considered less moral than two people who are living a lie in a marital façade behind which there is a psychological and spiritual separation?

How can we be sure that we love someone—or merely want him or her for selfish or sensual reasons? Obviously there is a great need to understand love. It is hoped that this book, in its total implication, will at least help to promote such understanding. But if we have been habitually insincere in the expression of our feelings, we may be unable to tell whether we love or not. We will think we love when we simply want another person for ourselves. How often "falling in love" is the sole basis upon which relationships build. The term may be more apt than we suspect, for it may well be a falling into sensuality and selfishness. Thomas à Kempis says that when a person seeks his own, he falls from love.

The "fall" may well be inevitable in any growing relationship. We are all spiritual beings, expressing ourselves in and through a physical body temple. The physical body and its drives and functions are very much a part of the wholeness that is us. It is so very important that we realize that any healthy marriage relationship must involve the whole of us, which means that there probably will come an opening up of the sexual element in the progressive growth toward the whole communion of self with self. At a certain introductory point we "fall in love." However, after the fall there must be a progressive rise in love in the evolution of the spiritual union. "Unless the Lord builds the house, those who build it labor in vain" (Ps. 127:1).

What is usually thought of as "being in love" may well be, at the outset, simply the desire to possess. This tends to blind us to pretense about the person's virtues, his or her beauties and capacities. It normally deprives us of the power of honest feelings, wrapping us in a fog of unreality. Perhaps it is in this context that Shakespeare says, "Love is blind."[2] It is not really love, of course, but a kind of euphoria that results from the "fall."

When we really love someone, we love the person in stark reality, refusing to shut our eyes to defects and actions. For to do that is to shut our eyes to needs. How can we be a true helpmate to another if we insist upon seeing him as a "knight in shining armor" or her as a "living doll"? True love is a peculiar kind of insight through which we see the wholeness which the person is—at the same time totally accepting the level on which he now expresses himself—without any delusion that the potential is a present reality. True love accepts the person who now is without qualifications, but with a sincere and unwavering commitment to help him to achieve his goals of self-unfoldment—which we may see better than he does. For this is a property of love by which we can judge its validity—the ability to see in another person something that no one, not even the person himself, sees with equal clarity.

In the transcendence of this kind of love—in which our beloved is not just the means of our fulfillment or security, but a living embryo of a diviner life to which we joyously give ourselves in support—the sexual relationship is one of the possible expressions of love, one of the means of support, one of the steps toward greater communion. It is neither something high and holy—something to venerate and idealize—nor is it something low and contemptible, something to be ashamed of. It is a beautiful function for the expression and consummation of the activity and energy of love.

Sex is too often made a thing apart, kept apart from the reality of life, mentioned only in whispers. When sex is considered as a "thing" in itself, even persons very much in love can be frustrated and confused, with their consummation of love dangerously inhibited, causing a physical separation that can and often does lead to divorce—even when two persons are "divinely intended" for each other. It is the result of ignorance about sex—when it is at times exalted romantically and at other times debased with feelings of contempt—when persons turn from love to sex as if they were two different things.

Whenever sex is singled out as something very special and wonderful or something base and terrible, it is made uncontrollable. This is what our society has done under the Puritanical influence. It has produced in most persons a chronic condition of quite unnatural exasperation.

Sex should be considered in the context of the whole man—as a very real part and process of the unity of all life. It should be a channel for the expression of total love. Of course, if it is to be lifted above the realm of the procreative biological process, it must come as a true feeling of oneness between a man and a woman which transcends egotism and selfish desires. It must come as an overflow of love which envelops two body temples with a transcendent experience of oneness.

In this kind of unity sex ceases to be an appetite, an addiction to sensuality, a want to be satisfied. It becomes a simple and natural and very beautiful means of communion. It is not just mutual self-satisfaction, for that is two persons using each other for their own gratification. In the context of pure love, this is impure and immoral. Love's fulfillment through a sexual experience is two persons filling each other full of the vital expression of love.

As the psychologist said, "There is no such thing as sex." Perhaps this concept needs to take root in our consciousness, so that we can begin to rise above the lifelong fragmentation of ourselves into complicated parts. Let us begin to deal with ourselves as whole persons, engaged in the growth experiences of loving and being loved, and making use of our sexuality; not as a thing in itself, but as a beautiful process of the communion of two persons, as persons, and not just as sex partners. Certainly this is an ideal toward the fulfillment of which every student of life should give his whole mind and heart in sincere effort, for *life is for loving*.

6. *The Healing Power of Love*

In our study of love in its many phases, it is doubtful that we have come up with anything close to a definition for love. Perhaps it is good that we haven't done so, for to define a thing is the simplest way to dispose of it. We could say, "Love is da-da-da-da," and that would end the discussion. The subject would be closed. Of course all we would have would be a hollow vessel, empty of all relevance, forever keeping us from the dynamics of love.

What we are doing is suggesting a few things that love is not. The Greek philosopher Zeno said that the most necessary part of learning is to unlearn our errors. We have so many erroneous thoughts about love. We have thought of it as an emotion, as sentimentality, as a sexual experience, and as something we fall into or out of in a way as unpredictable as are the changes in the weather.

The poet reminds us that we may not see the wind but we can see the rustle of the leaves. And we cannot really see love, the activity of transcendence. The gentle smile on the face of a mother nursing her infant at her breast, or the confident and courageous air of a man going off to work feeling the supportive influence of a loving wife are but two of many evidences of its presence. Love is life expressing its fullness, the wholeness of man in fruition. Under the sustaining influence of love, the physical body is always at its best. It is probably true that more people are sick from lack of love in their lives than from all other causes put together.

When Jesus repeatedly emphasized such things as love one another; love your neighbor as yourself; love your enemy; go the second mile, He was dealing with the healing power of love. He wasn't saying that you should be loving and forgiving because other people deserve it. Certainly He knew the malicious intent with which others could treat you. He was saying that you can't afford to dwell on what others do, but must guard well how you react to what they do. He knew that you cannot afford not to dwell in the fullness of love, which is the key to health and healing.

Man is so created that he cannot survive in health and wellness without love. We are created in and of love. To deny the flow of love in us is to deny the reality of our being. To live with anything less than love contaminates the wholeness that we are, frustrating our potential for the creative experience of life in its fullness. The healthy and vital life actually defines and reveals what love is. Jesus said, "He who has seen me has seen the Father" (John 14:9). In Him we could see life in its fullness, and love in its most complete expression. And both are the outpicturing of the inexplicable process we call God.

On the other hand, anything less than love in the mind and heart of man causes tension and stress. Hatred, bitterness, and even unfriendliness frustrates the healing process, interfering with the normal renewal of cells and the flow of vital healing fluids. More than this, consciousness, in moods that are unloving, actually creates harmful fluids and even toxic poisons in the body.

Consider, for instance, the person who receives a telegram stating that a close relative is dead. Suddenly the person mysteriously manufactures and releases something that was not present before—a quantity of saline liquid called "tears." The tears were not there in the system before the bad news came, save in potential. Crying is not like turning on a tap and running off a liquid stored in some reservoir behind the eyes. Yet in a few moments there is brought into existence enough liquid to soak a small handkerchief.

This same process is involved in the creation of fluids that eat at the lining of the stomach and poison various parts of the system. A young mother is often told to encourage happy and contented and loving thoughts while she is feeding her baby at her breast, because her feelings can actually change the chemical constitution of her breast milk. There are known records of a mother engaging in heated arguments and indulging in emotions of anger and hate and bitterness—while feeding the baby—in which the baby actually died of poisonous breast-milk toxins.

This is an interesting concept of psychosomatic medicine. Conditions of disease, hitherto regarded as physiogenic, can be set up, not by infective sources outside the body, but through the action of the emotions which release or create toxins within the body—actually altering the chemical contents of some of the body's important fluids.

The body contains bacteria which are healthy and friendly to the system, the so-called saprophytes. But a change in the chemical composition of the fluid in which these benign bacteria live may possibly convert friendly bacteria into hostile ones, saprophytes into parasites. It is conjectured by some researchers that all pathogenic microbes at some period may have originated from the microbes that were saprophytic upon the body surfaces, and which were converted into disease organisms by negative emotions. This would seem to parallel the ideas of Luther Burbank who believed that the most foul-smelling weed was simply a degenerate plant that could be reclaimed with proper cultivation.

Many persons have puzzled over the idea of God as the origin of all life—because of the inescapable conclusion that He must also have caused or created disease germs and illness. But there is another much more likely conclusion: that God, the creative process, makes all bacteria good, and that it is negative emotions of anger or worry or fear or hate that have poisoned the system and brought hostile organisms into being —in a kind of reverse application of Paul's "Be ye transformed by the renewing of the mind." How insightful was that writer of the Bible who said, "God made man upright, but they have sought out many inventions" (Eccles. 7:29, ASV).

This is not to say that love is physical or chemical, but that this mysterious force has a measurable influence upon the balance of the physical system, that without the harmonizing power of love, the basic forces of the system run rampant and actually become self-destructive.

However, love is not simply a force acting within and upon the body.

Certainly it does act on the physical form, and the very skin tissues are alive and vibrant in the person who is sincerely loving and well-beloved. But there is a radiance of this love that is a very real harmonizing factor in the atmosphere. Extensive experiments have proved that plants grow faster and better in a home with a loving atmosphere. And the lack of love or the actual emanation of hatred and its related negative emotions can have as much influence on man and nature as polluted air. It is likely that the means will eventually be devised by which we could check the vibrations of a room or office or plant, as with a Geiger counter, to determine if living or working conditions are healthful—or if there is pollution caused by an absence of the purifying force of love.

In my book, *Unity of All Life*,[1] I tell of a home to which a doctor had been called to examine a seriously ill child. He felt an oppressive atmosphere immediately on entering the house. As he looked at the parents he found anger, suspicion, bitterness, and hatred. He examined the child and found every evidence of a serious heart and circulatory deficiency. He told the parents that the child would not live six months unless something were done. They said they would do anything.

The doctor told the distraught parents that medicine probably could not help, but perhaps love could. He talked to them about their discord. It came out that a relative, an in-law, had come between them, creating a bitter problem. The doctor told them that they would have to make a decision: Did they want these ill feelings, or did they want their child? They could not have both. He left them to think about it.

About a week later the doctor returned. He immediately sensed a fresh air of love. He examined the child, and there was evidence of a return to normalcy. The parents thanked him for saving their lives—and the life of their child. The mysterious energy of love had worked its miracle.

It is a terrible burden to dislike people or to be involved in bitterness or hatred or condemnation. Such feelings cover a perpetual pain in our own heart. We may justify ourselves by saying, "But you should know what he has done to me," or, "After the way they treated me . . ." And we might even add, "Of course I am disturbed and bitter. You would be too, if you were in my place." This reflects the all-too-common attitude that life is lived from outside-in. We are happy if we are surrounded by happy experiences. We are upset if conditions are disturbing. It is a precarious way to live. However, it is the way most people do live and think—which is precisely why there is such a high incidence in our Western culture of indigestion and heart and circulatory ailments. Certainly there are disturbing conditions in the world. We can keep posted on them by hearing the news "every hour on the hour." If we are disturbable, it will be like taking a constant dose of arsenic in our coffee.

How much better to know that life is lived from inside-out, to set the tone for the day, each morning, by remembering, "In the beginning . . . love." Love is or can be a creative force at the root of all things. We need to determine that, no matter what the day brings, we will identify with love. In this way we will easily relate to all that is lovely and we will react to all things in thoughts that are loving. Then we will know what Jesus meant when He said, "In the world you have tribulations; but . . . I have overcome the world" (John 16:33).

The reason we are overcome by "the world," and thus turn from positive to negative emotions, is that we are living in the consciousness of divisiveness instead of unity. Not realizing oneness, not knowing that "I am my brother and my brother is me," we see our life in conflict and competition with other persons. We think they can hurt us, harm us, or take our good from us. We are defensive and fearful, creating walls to keep them out, but succeeding only in keeping the healing power of love dammed up within us.

The wise student of life will realize that any evidence of anger, hate, bitterness, envy, or criticism in his own nature are danger signals that should never be ignored. We need to start loving quickly, just as we would hurry to put an antidote in our stomach if we had inadvertently taken a poison. Jesus knew this when He said, "Agree with your adversary quickly." He wasn't saying that we should be passive and meek, letting anyone and everyone trample upon us and our rights. The adversaries, the only things that can hurt or harm us, are always the adverse thoughts of our own mind. We have caused them and only we can change them. We must start loving and blessing the persons, even those who we feel may have "despitefully used us," so that we can get back into the stream of positive love energy, without which our body temple cannot long survive.

One woman told me the story about her relationship with her mother. It had been a very poor relationship through many years. They spoke, and they were normally "polite," but that was about all. In later years the mother, whose whole life had been plagued with arthritis and various nervous disorders, came under her complete care. During this period the woman, resisting the added cost and responsibility, began to experience a serious deterioration of her own health. Eventually the mother had to be hospitalized. The daughter was at the hospital arranging the stay, when the mother poured forth a venom of bitterness, saying that all her troubles began with the day this daughter was born. She flatly stated that the total cause of her illness was the daughter.

Of course, the daughter was crushed. We say "of course," because in human consciousness it seems to be the normal reaction to be hurt by another's taunts or slights. This woman walked the streets, wondering how she could make her mother love her—all the while sensing in her own physical body some of the serious ailments that had long plagued her mother. Then, in the wee hours of the night, as she sat crying on the edge of her bed, she suddenly remembered a statement she had heard years before: "Divine Love never fails. . . . If only you can love enough, you can never be hurt."

Suddenly she realized that she *was* being hurt, so it must follow that she had not been loving enough. She saw that she should not be worrying about why her mother did not love her. She should be giving more love to her mother. She began blessing her mother, sending waves of love— and in that consciousness she went off to sleep. The next day she sent her mother some flowers with a note that simply said, "I love you." She sent loving letters each day, and began to feel only love for her mother in her thoughts. The beautiful thing was that her own physical problems cleared up almost instantly. While engaged in this constant experience of love for her mother, she felt the warm glow of love within her, giving her peace, and joy, and a renewed self-respect. More than this, she discovered a new depth within her that opened the door to whole new dimensions of self-realization.

This woman said she never saw her mother again, for she died some days later. But "enough love" had not failed. Before her death, the mother found the strength to sit up in bed and write a note to her daughter: "Oh, if you could only know what your love and your letters have meant to me. I do not know what made me cruel to one I love so much. Perhaps I can explain it when I am stronger. Please forgive me, know how proud of you I am, and that I love you—Mama."

This mother had a block within her that had kept her love dammed up through much of her life, causing frustration and years of physical affliction. And this same frustration had been visited upon the second generation—at least for awhile. But love built a bridge—bringing freedom and release—at least to the daughter who could now go forward to a new expression of wholeness through love. And perhaps it brought freedom and release also to the mother—in a healing process that transcends even death, opening the way for her soul to go forward to new experiences of unfoldment along life's eternal way.

Traditionally, love has been closely associated with the physical organ of the heart. There is no physiological basis for this, for much that is involved in love may actually come through the cerebrum. But the heart is the most influenced by love, or by the frustration of love in the variety of negative emotions. Certainly the heart and circulatory system are the first to respond to this frustration. Among the common causes of heart trouble: fear, sudden shock, brooding over financial or other losses, the belief in strain, hurry, being easily hurt—eating our heart out. We do this because of a lack of the feeling of oneness which love promotes.

Of course, love is not generated by the heart. As we have said, love does not begin in us and end in the object of our love. Love is the action of divine law, an energy force that flows through us, but which begins in the Infinite Creative Source and has no end. The heart is simply the tangible manifestation of the divine heart-idea in God-mind. However, this means that a perfect heart is the plan and creative intention of God. So-called heart disease must originate in the frustration of love, or in the toxicity caused by an absence of love.

Charles Fillmore insisted that a strong feeling of love allowed to flow out through the heart to all persons and all living things, coupled with a sense of loving gratitude for the truth of the divinity of man and the

Fatherhood of God, felt strongly every morning on awakening and every night on retiring, would cure any so-called heart trouble.

If there seems to be a weakness, even an impairment, of the heart, do not dwell on the thought of weakness. No matter what road you may be taking in treatment—medical, nutritional, or physio-therapeutic— never refer to "my weak heart" or "my poor circulation." The body is your servant not your master. You are the master! You must rule—but with a loving hand. Praise your body. Talk to its various parts in loving ways. If you have been in the habit of dissipating your positive energy by criticizing and condemning your bodily ills, start a new program of love. Stand in front of the mirror for ten minutes every morning, before you have dressed, and talk to your body gently and lovingly. Bless your hands and feet, your lungs and stomach, your muscles and joints. And especially—bless your heart!

It is written, "I will give them a heart to know that I am the Lord" (Jer. 24:7). We have all been given the heart to know God, to attune ourselves with the Infinite Life and Love of Spirit. The physical heart is the manifest expression of a transcendent force—the great heart of God, "the one great heart that beats for all." Actually, there is a counterpart energy and pattern that beats your heart. This has been proved through some interesting experiments in the biological quest into "force fields of life." Dwell on this counterpart heart idea in spirit. Let the transcendence of love beat your heart, and flow through it in a loving vibration that heals your body and establishes harmonious relations with the world.

There is a strong race suggestion that one of the symptoms of "growing old" is the weakening of the heart, the hardening of the arteries, and the deterioration of the body's vital centers. This is one of the errors that must be unlearned. Life cannot grow old. God is life—in us, through us, expressing as us. The need is to "let God be God in us." Let life *be* life in us. And let love *be* love in us, for love is the energizer and harmonizer of life.

What is called "old age" has not come about through any toxicity of age itself. Age is not a disease but an experience in consciousness. The poisons that may deteriorate the cells of the body in the aging process come not from life or even from a supposed waning of life through the accumulation of birthdays. These poisons are created by the negativity of thought and emotion—the belief in aging, and the frustration of love —through a sense of loneliness and separation.

Treat your body temple to life! Give yourself a daily youthfulness and beauty treatment. Say to and for yourself, "I am *in* love with life. Life is *in* love with me. In love there is beauty and wholeness and the full, free expression of abundant life. This day is my birthday, for I am reborn in the awareness of the love that is me. I celebrate myself in the transcendent experience of love!"

It is strange how we get out of tune with the harmonizing power of love! Living at the circumference of our being, we become immersed in the consciousness of materiality and the pressures of conformity and competition, with the resulting breakdown of communication between even those who are close to us. Finally, trying to escape the problems of separation and the prison of aloneness, we fall into the trap of such tragedies as alcoholism.

One man who was generous and good by nature, found himself alienated from his family and from the reality of himself by an overinvolvement in the world of materiality. "Living beyond his spiritual means," he began drinking to excess and finally was trapped in alcoholism. After a series of minor heart ailments, a doctor finally told him that his heart was "all shot to pieces," that there was little hope of recovery, and that he had better get his affairs in order for he had but a short time to live.

He was in the hospital after a long weekend of drinking that had ended in a total blackout. He lay there, terribly depressed. His wife had already taken the children and had gone back to her people. He was at the end of the road. There was nothing left to live for. As the doctor left the room he reached for a bottle he had secreted nearby. When a nurse removed it from his reach, he cried out with an oath, "What a mess! Business all shot to pieces, heart all shot to pieces, my whole life shot to pieces!" Then, with his chin sinking on his breast, he pleaded with the nurse, "Give me something to end it all!"

She answered, "All right, I will." The man's head shot up in astonishment. "What I will give you is a promise of God, and God never goes back on a promise. Here it is: 'Behold, I have loved you with an everlasting love.' So God is a force of love in you that can give you a spirit of mastery, of understanding, and of self-control. God also says, 'A new heart will I give you, and a new spirit will I put within you.' All right, accept that! God has given *you* a new heart and a new spirit."

The nurse then went on to tell him that love was a mighty healing force in him that could heal and renew and restore his heart, repair his whole body, and remake his life. At first the man was resentful; yet in his heart he knew that the advice was correct. It was difficult to admit that the problem was really within himself, for the male ego did not want to let go. But he had an awful lot of time on his hands and a lot of "sheer necessity." He was at last ready to try anything.

So the man began to meditate on love, the totality of love, flowing into and through his heart. He imagined the divine heart-idea exerting an influence upon his heart, actually beating his heart, reshaping and remolding it, influencing the renewal of its cells. He talked lovingly to his heart, almost as if it were another person: "You are a good heart, for you have done a pretty great job in putting up with me through all the years of abuse. You are one with the one great heart of God, beating steadily and freely, pumping the life force into and through you and out to every cell of my body. You can do what you need to do because you have the potential of newness of life within you. I am *in* love with you, and you are *in* love with me. We are *in* love together, therefore we are whole."

The next time the doctor examined the man's heart, he was astonished at the change. The doctor said that if he continued to show the kind of improvement that he had he would be ready for service again within a month. The man replied confidently, "Doc, I don't think it will take that long. You see, I have Someone Else working for me, too." Eventually the man was completely healed, and he went on to rebuild his life, his self-respect, his business, and his family.

"In the beginning . . . love!" Love is the foundation of the whole and complete life. Affirm often, "I am *in* love with life. Life is *in* love with me." Bless your body. And, since for so many of us it has become the symbolic center of both life and love, bless your heart. The statement, "Bless your heart!" is both an excellent salutation and greeting for others and a marvelous treatment for yourself. It is like saying, "God-love in me salutes the center of God-love in you." In blessing the heart of others, you are relating on the level of transcendental love, which means you are engaged in the wellness-sustaining activity of love within yourself.

Here is an excellent treatment for your heart, and through the radiant action of your heart in the full expression of love, for every part of your mind, body, and affairs:

Blessed is your heart. The pure love and life of God pulsate through it in perfect rhythm and order. It is cleansed of all misunderstanding, inharmony, impurity, and disease. In the beginning . . . love! It is this cosmic energy of love that circulates your blood. It is the harmonious action of the creative power of love that gives perfect respiration, perfect digestion, and perfect elimination. In the beginning . . . love! Your heart responds to the activity of divine law by acting in perfect unison with the even, regular, firm, powerful action of life. In the beginning . . . love! Your heart is not the source of love, but love is the energizer of your heart and of the life of your whole body. You are in tune with the one great heart that beats for all, and with the Infinite flow of Divine Love that sustains all. You are filled and thrilled with love, your heart is aglow with vitalizing life, and your whole being is established in the wholeness of love which you are. You are a wonderful, peaceful, and "loveful" child of the Most High.

7. The Work of Your Life

One of the greatest needs of man is the discovery of life as an integrated whole. From earliest times he has sensed this wholeness, which has led to varied acts of worship (the attempt to remember his worth-ship), to ceremonies of communion (the involvement in oneness), and to the establishment of whole religions (acting out this oneness as a way of life). Of course, not all devotees caught this vision. Many of them, as Bliss Carman sings, are "praising God on Sunday, but they are all right on Monday; for it's just a little habit they've acquired."

In no area of life is the need for wholeness more profound than in the work of our lives. For work, when dealt with out of the context of the whole man, is a painful process that we engage in "by the sweat of our brow." We have a tendency to enter into our work life as if it were a life sentence from which we might ultimately retire as time off for good behavior. We talk about entering the "labor market" as if we sell ourselves and our services in exchange for the wherewithal to exist. We often describe our job with the casual statement, "Oh, it's a living!" Actually, it may be a drab existence. It certainly cannot be the "life more abundant" that Jesus idealized.

The work of our life should not be simply a *doing;* it should be a BEING. We have a way of asking a person, "What do you do for a living?" He may say, "Oh, I am a baker, or a bricklayer, or a teacher, or a merchant." But actually, if he could but know the wholeness of life, he would respond, "I let God be God in me." And because God is love, he is created in and of God. Thus he could also say, *"Life is for loving! My true work is to let love be love in me, for 'work is love made visible!' "*

Emerson had this sense of the wholeness of life. Again and again he urged, no matter what your work, let it be your own. No matter what your occupation, let what you are doing be organic, let it be in your bones. In this way, he believed, you will open the door by which the affluence of heaven and earth shall stream into you.

When work is something we *do,* it is not really ours. Certainly it is not *us.* For I can only *be* me and you can only *be* you. Our chief business in life must be the "express business," expressing or pressing out into visibility that divine activity that is Being being us. Jesus had this cosmic insight: "And I must work the works of Him that sent me" (John 9:4 AV). Thus the work of our life is the *outworking* of the reality of our being.

Kahlil Gibran, in his work, *The Prophet,* has an amazing insight into the work of your life. He says, "When you work you fulfill a part of earth's furthest dream, assigned to you when that dream was born, and in keeping yourself with labor, you are in truth loving life, and to love life through labor is to be intimate with life's inmost secret."[1] When you are "intimate with life's inmost secret," you are intimate with the seed of your divine nature. Your work becomes your outworking, your "calling." The word "vocation" comes from the Latin "voco," which means "I call." The creative process is calling, singing its song in us and *as* us. When we become attuned to the symphony of life, we sing the song with joy. But the work we do or the song we sing is not ours, but the "will of Him who sent us." Thus our work is easy, and it is successful, for it is "love made visible."

Gibran says, "When you work with love you bind yourself to yourself, and to one another, and to God."[2] Work then becomes a growth experience, an outworking of the "inner splendor" of our divine potential. To approach work, any work, in this attitude, is to see it as a kind of worship. Certainly, it will bring an increase in self-respect or a deep feeling of worth-ship.

So much time and attention is given to finding the right work for our life. Usually it is from a totally superficial point of view relating to our exterior orientation toward life. The emphasis, thus, is upon work that is lucrative, interesting, secure, with the most opportunities for advancement and the increase of personal power. How much more important to emphasize "being the right person"! As someone once affirmed, "Wherever I am, there let me BE!" One of the greatest causes of frustration and mental and physical breakdowns can be found in those lives that are committed to doing the things that make for money and power, rather than to being the channel for the expression of the creative power of love. In no way does this imply the renunciation of prosperity and success. What it does mean is that the one is devoted to "making a living" while the other is joyously engaged in "making a life." The one achieves his rewards at the *expense* of his life while the other enjoys the fruits of his creativity at the *expanse* of his life.

The greatest need is not to find the right work, but to discover the right attitude. It is not simply finding a work to which to devote our lives, but rather experiencing work as the overflow of our love of life. In the consciousness of the fullness of love as the reality of our being, our work, whatever it may be, will be as an outworking of an innate activity. It will be this, even if we undertake a job that seems otherwise foreign to us, for we will transform the work and lift it up into a transcendent thing by our attitude of love.

Gibran says, "Work is love made visible. And if you cannot work with love but only with distaste, it is better that you should leave your work and sit at the gate of the temple and take alms of those who work with joy. For if you bake bread with indifference, you bake a bitter bread that feeds but half man's hunger. And if you grudge the crushing of the grapes, your grudge distills a poison in the wine. . . ."[3] It is interesting that Gibran makes the same point about negative attitudes poisoning the things you make in your work, as we mentioned happening when a mother fed a baby in bitterness and thus actually injected toxic poisons into the milk. If you do not love your work, you are cut off from the source of creativity. Love is an integrating force that unites the worker with the work, and that lifts the work into a continuation of the Creator, saying in the beginning, "Let there be!" Work that is done without love is work that is depleting; it becomes an exhausting drudgery. The hardest part of any job whether it be mental or physical is the resistance that the worker has toward it. The hardest work we can do is that which is done without love. It is like driving the car with the brakes on. Or more correctly, it is like pushing the car with our own power rather than engaging the gear which lets the two hundred horses of the motor do the work.

You may say, "But I am not happy with my work; how can I love it?" This is a common complaint, leading to frustrations on jobs, and to the frustrating experience of job-hopping in the quest for the kind of work that is happy and interesting and conducive to loving. However, if we are not happy with our work, we need to check up on ourselves, the way we are working, and the attitudes we are holding toward our work. When we feel that our work is beneath us, it may be that we do not love and respect ourselves, and that we are trying to find in a job that which we can find only in ourselves by changing our thoughts.

If we awaken on a Monday morning begrudging the need to get back to work, it may well be that our work has become an escape from ourselves. It is an alternative to boredom, a means by which we may be set free for a few hours from the prison of our aloneness. The "Monday morning blues" may be a soliloquy of self-disrespect for selling our soul "for a mess of pottage." From deep within us there is an urge to "come up higher," to transcend the burdensome *doing* through the loving experience of *being*. Monday morning is a good time to make a new beginning by meditating on the ideal, *Life is for loving:*

I am a creature of love, created in and of love. I am in love with life, and life is in love with me. I am the work of God made visible through His love. And my work is to let this love express in me and as me, and to let it overflow through the work of my hands and the creativity of my mind. I love to work because my work is the continuation of God's work in me. As I do my work with love, the activity of God works through me to make my work easy, joyous, and fulfilling. And my work will bring prosperity and success to me in abundant ways. However, I will not let these ends be the objects of my work—only the spilling over of the fullness of love in me being made visible.

One of man's pitfalls in the world of materiality is this thing called "money." Paul said, "for the love of money is the root of all kinds of evil" (I Tim. 6:10, ASV). Of course it is not money that is evil, but the attitude toward money. Because we live in a world where money is the basis of the economy, we will always require it as a medium of exchange. The question is, How will we think about it? If we love and work for money, its accumulation will be as a millstone around our neck. Our happiness in life will be proportionate to the amounts of money and possessions that we accumulate. But we will not *have* them—they will have us. On the other hand, if we work to let the divine outworking of love flow through us, money will be a symbol of that loving exchange within us. We will have money in abundance to care for all our needs, but it will never become a burden. We will have all things needed to make our life rich, but they will never possess us.

Dorothy Sayers makes the observation that the habit of thinking about work as something we do to make money is so ingrained in us that we can hardly imagine what a difference it would be to think of it instead in terms of work done. She says it would mean approaching our work with the attitude we hold toward our hobbies or leisure activities. We need to think of a particular work, not in terms of "What will it pay?" but "Is it good?" And of a person, not "How much does he make?" but "What is his work worth?" Of employment, not "How much a week?" but "Will it permit me to work out of the fullness of my faculties?" Work, she says, is not primarily a thing one does to live but the thing one lives to do.

Now, if we think of work as a way to make money, soon we will think of it as a necessary alternative to getting money for nothing. Often work is referred to as "easy money"! Which in turn gives rise to the attitude of working just enough to get by. In this consciousness the worker begrudges the demand for extra work and even makes his own demands for extra pay. It could even be said that the modern corollary of "going the extra mile" is getting two-mile pay for one-mile work. From here it is but a step beyond to the practice of working just long enough to qualify for unemployment compensation, where one is paid for no work at all. Of course, this is a total lack of balance, completely out of tune with the harmony of the universe.

There are those who condemn the move on the part of government to require some work from all able-bodied persons in order to receive welfare assistance. But government that gives something for nothing misleads and fails the individual in need. There is a universal law of "give and receive," and the person in need has an even greater need to give, to open the process of the creative flow through investment of himself in acts of giving through work.

As we have been saying again and again, the person who needs love needs to relate to the reality of himself *in* love, and thus to become loving in his relationships in the world. In the same way, when we need work, we need to "give ourselves away." For every person has a great work to do, something that the creative process is seeking to do through and *as* him. He also has a great need to let this work come forth. As Nehemiah replied to the voices that would lure him away from his high place of commitment, "I am doing a great work and I cannot come down" (Neh. 6:3). The "great work" is to "work the works of Him that sent me." This is the work that is to be done, even if there is no place of employment. The attitude, then, should be, "God has a work for me to do that no one else can do but me. I am *in* love with God, and God is *in* love with me. In this oneness of love, I let His process flow through me, guiding me, directing me, fulfilling me, prospering me."

Work is too often thought of in terms of receiving. We need to form the habit of thinking "give" in all that we do. "Think *give* instead of *get!*" In this consciousness living becomes a giving, loving is giving, and working is giving. Working is simply letting God *be* God in us. God has no other hands through which to create than man's hands. As the poet puts it, "God could not create Antonio Stradivari's violins without Antonio."[4] Of course, it is also true that Antonio could not create the violin without the idea of the violin in Divine Mind. Antonio, then, was simply a midwife to assist in giving birth to the violin that bears his name.

It is when a person remembers that he has a salary to receive and forgets that he has a creative expression of love to give that he builds to an inevitable crisis. He is like a plant cut off from its roots. The cut flower may flourish for awhile in beauty and fragrance, but it is already fading toward decay and death. On the other hand, when a person is earnestly set on being useful, he is in a country where he can dig anywhere and strike oil. One who is unemployed may frantically look for work, but he may be unconsciously thinking only of getting on a payroll somewhere. Whenever he stops thinking of "getting," and of the need to "get," and begins looking for opportunities to give, though the experience may lead to a complete change in the work of his life, he will be drawn toward or will draw to him opportunities for service that will challenge the greatest release of his potentialities and become the means of filling the urgent need of others. And this is the formula for demonstrating prosperity and success.

Today the economists and politicians are pondering the ills of our economy. The "wage and price freeze" was a frantic attempt to deal with the symptoms. But since it did not deal with the real cause of the problem, it could bring no long-range cure any more than an aspirin can cure the cause of a headache. It could be said that one of the greatest ills of our society is that we have lost the consciousness of the labor of love. We may well be in the midst of a great depression of worker attitudes.

A new insight into the reality of love may be the answer. The attitude so typical of the modern worker is "good enough." This leads to a progressive deterioration of the quality of work and of any pursuit of excellence. If we are engaged in a relationship of love, there can be no withholding or restriction. We love out of the fullness of love that we are, and there can be no "alteration when it alteration finds." We love, and we love more, and yet we love still more. Simply because we are *in* love.

In the work of our life, if we begin with the realization that we are created in and of love, then our very work becomes a love affair with life. And the giving of ourselves to our work is unstinting and total. It is "Good, better, best, I'll never let it rest, till my good is better and my better is best." The work that is done is the projection of the self as it manifests God. Thus, if we do less than our best we dishonor God and show a total disrespect toward ourselves.

In mature self-love we know that if a thing is worth doing at all, it is worth doing at the very fullest of our ability. But we know that it is not done by our own power but through our willingness to let the creative flow use us. Work then becomes satisfying and fulfilling, for it is done out of the fullness of our love and in complete respect for the person we now are and the divinity we are unfolding.

In a very real sense work is the continuation of the divine effort that made the man. Because we are created in and of love, our work, if it is to be done at the *expanse* of our nature and not at its expense, must become the outworking of an inward creative process and the overflow of the fullness of love. To work in this consciousness is to work with inspiration, to give birth to amazing ideas, and to labor without fatigue or boredom.

The classic example is Michelangelo, who approached a block of marble, not with the thought that he would create a statue, but with the vision of a "Boy David" within the stone. His vision of work was to release that which was already done in the ideal. This is what Jesus had in mind when He said, "The Father worketh, even until now, and I work" (John 5:17, ASV). My work is simply to become a channel for the manifestation of that which has already been done by the Father.

Thus for Michelangelo there could be no ego hangups with the result, and no strain in the creative process. A particular work might require a month or a lifetime of tedious effort; but it was a work of love being made visible, so he worked without fatigue or discouragement. We might say, "But look at the rewards and acclaim his work has brought to him or to his memory down through the years!" However, no compensation that came to him in his lifetime and no plaudits accorded to his work in the years since could in any way compare with the exhilaration that he felt while he was tuned in on the flow.

While Michelangelo was loving the "Boy David" into existence, he was loving himself and loving God. And, in a way beyond knowing, he was being loved by God, by life, and by this offspring of his own creative genius. The classic figure of the "Boy David" as it can be seen in Florence today is Michelangelo affirming, "I let God be God in me, I let love be love in me." It is truly love made visible!

Life is for loving! The good worker must be a good lover, and good work will always be the creation of a mind and heart in tune with the

Infinite through the unifying process of love. And if we love without end, we will work without interruptions of layoffs or unemployment. Even the termination of one job will simply be the opportunity to love more, to live more, to grow more. And in growing will come new work and new joys of giving.

There is a concept that is heard frequently through the Bible: "Wait on the Lord." "Those that wait upon the Lord, they shall inherit the earth" (Ps. 37:9, AV). The word "wait" comes from the Hebrew word "qavah" (kaw-vah), which means "to bind together." To wait upon the Lord is to integrate ourselves with the power and potential of our spiritual nature. And the one integrating force is *love*.

Before undertaking any project in the work of our life, we should wait on the Lord by taking a moment consciously to get into the flow of the creative process. In quiet meditation we can return to the principle, "In the beginning . . . love!" We can then remember that we are integral parts of the whole, and that the whole of Infinite Mind is seeking to say and do something quite unique and special through us. When we work in this consciousness we work with the fullest of integrity. And in the working we become integrated with our fellow man, both through attracting their collaboration as co-workers and also by their cooperation in buying and selling the products of our labor.

"Waiting on the Lord" we become integrated in a very special way with the creative flow within us. We are then in the position to realize the wholeness of our life and the fullness of our love. Our work then becomes a dynamic opportunity to love and to be enriched by loving— and prosperity and success, in the way that is in keeping with our highest ideals, comes easily. We are then ready to be intimate "with life's inmost secret" by loving life through our work.

Established in the consciousness that *Life is for loving*, we will go off to work in the morning with the eagerness of the lover going to meet his beloved, and we will engage in our work in the kind of mutual sharing that lovers experience together. We will return from work at the close of the day with the joyous feeling that we have given much of ourselves to our work and have received much from our work. But in the giving and receiving the greatest joy will be in knowing that we are in tune with "life's procession, that marches in majesty and proud submission towards the infinite."[5]

8. *Man's Love Affair With God*

Some of the clearest insights into the mysterious cosmic energy of love have been revealed by Teilhard de Chardin, the Catholic priest-paleontologist. In his concept of the whole universe and the whole man he found love to be an attraction exercised upon each conscious element by the Center of the Universe, "the call toward the great union, whose attainment is the only real business in nature." [1]

There is a Center within every person and a great Center within the universe. Teilhard refers to this as Omega—the cosmic point of total synthesis. And he sees love as the energy that seeks first to lift each person into wholeness, the totalization of his true self; and second, it seeks to bring each person into harmony with all other persons with whom he may be involved—and all this out of a communion or oneness with "the conscious Center of total convergence." [2]

Now the obvious and very exciting implication of all this is that love is not something that comes and goes by the changing moods of man, something we can fall into or out of or feel strain or drain through expression, or something that can ever be depleted. Love is an energy force that emanates as naturally from the center of us as radiation from Uranium. We are always "loveful."

Living at the surface of experience the energy of love may be felt simply as an emotion or as sensuality, or even as a drive for materiality. We may experience it chiefly as a restless hunger, a passionate desire for fulfillment. We may thus be impelled to a continuous search in the world "out there" for conquests and achievements and possessions, while what our heart really longs for is to be united in a conscious sense of oneness with the heart of the universe.

It is often said that the greatest need of man is to be loved, which is true. But it is a mistake to think that this need for love can be filled by others. Our yearning for love can be satisfied only by touching the Love Center within us. It is a "remembering" that "In the beginning . . . love" is the root of our being. The key to developing a consciousness of this love so that the energy of love may flow easily in and through us is in meditation, "Man's love affair with God."

Charles Fillmore once said, "One should make it a practice to meditate regularly on the love idea in Universal Mind, with the prayer, 'Divine Love, manifest thyself in me.' This produces a positive love-current, which, when sent forth with power, will break up opposing thoughts and render them null and void. . . . The love current is not a projection of the will, it is a setting free of a natural equalizing, harmonizing force that in most people has been dammed up by human limitation."[3]

Meditation is a subject that is both popular and greatly confused in modern times. To the Eastern mind it comes natural because the religious conditioning of people of the East is more inner-centered. Western religion has been centered in ritual and ceremony and wordy prayers. The follower of Judaism and Christianity, for instance, has had little experience in the withinness of spiritual seeking. His God has always been "out there" or "up there," and his prayers have been a reaching out and up, an attempt to relate to or communicate with a Deity who is much like an absentee landlord of the world.

Thus, the tendency in attempts at meditation is to try to experience inner communion with the same kind of tense reaching. As Teilhard puts it, "The presence is so universal and we are so surrounded and transfixed by it—there is no room to fall down and adore it, even within ourselves."[4] The goal is not to reach something, even to reach *for* something. It is letting go of the very desire to reach. There is really nowhere to go, nothing to do. We simply get ourselves out of the way and *let* the transcendence of us become the living reality of us.

Plotinus had an amazingly simple and yet extremely dynamic insight. He was probably one of the very first persons to conceive of man as being at the center of a totally supportive universe. He suggests that we let the soul banish all that disturbs it and the body let go of its tensions, and then think of Spirit as streaming, pouring, rushing, and shining into us from all sides while we stand quiet. In other words, *God is seeking us!*

Meditation is an experience in loving and being loved at the Center of us. This Center is not a place to go but a level of consciousness to feel. In this consciousness we love God and God loves us. There is no question of the latter, for—"I have loved you with an everlasting love." Our need is to accept it, to experience it, to bubble over with it. It is a consciousness that we are *in* love with God, and God is *in* love with us. And this sense of oneness in love "is the only real business of nature."

There are many techniques for meditation, which we will not attempt to describe or outline in this study—partly because of lack of space. But chiefly because we want to emphasize that meditation is not a mental practice, but an awareness that takes place in the heart. It is essentially an experience in and of love. It is an awakening and unfolding of our true nature—by love. Just as a flower unfolds in the rays of the sun, so the heart center opens through daily meditation and the practice of the presence of Divine Love.

When we feel the emotion of love, it is customary for the face to light up. The constant experience of transcendental love imparts to the face and to the whole being a spiritual radiance. The smile becomes alight with spiritual beauty. The smiling face is not only beautiful and joyful —it is "loveful."

Why not put on a smile as a preparation for meditation? By the law of reversibility could the smile not provide a vessel to be filled? Close your eyes for a moment. Smile. You do not really have to have something to smile about. Just let your face relax, and let the corners of your mouth turn up. Think of the smile as a vessel with its own form and shape and character. Now recall that the Spirit is "streaming, pouring, rushing, and shining into (you) from all sides while (you) stand quiet." Don't try to feel anything or do anything or reach for anything. Just be still with that smile held out as a cup to be filled. You will suddenly sense the "joy of the Lord" welling up within you and pouring into you, filling and justifying the smile. This kind of joy is the emanation of the cosmic energy of love. Let the warmth of that love sweep over you. Feel it, glory in it, give thanks for it!

This is not so much a technique in meditation as it is an exercise in experiencing the flow and overflow of God's love in you. But then, perhaps that is what meditation is. The great Indian master, Aurobindo, whose followers have evolved so many and varied concepts and techniques of meditation, used to tell his students that it was not necessary to show them how to meditate, and that what was needed would come of itself if they were open and sincere.

Perhaps the great prerequisite to meditation, or to engaging in the "love affair with God," is the conviction that there is a Center within you and within the universe, and that at that Center of convergence with the Infinite within you, your self is the emanation or image-likeness of God, and thus totally good. Charles Fillmore puts it thusly: "There is a divine goodness at the root of all existence. . . . No man is so lowly but that at the touch of its secret spring this divine goodness may be brought to light in him. . . . This goodness sleeps in the recesses of every mind and comes forth when least expected."⁵

There is little point in going to a bank for a withdrawal unless you know that you have an account there with adequate deposits. There is no purpose in engaging in meditation unless you believe that God is a Presence that *is* present, unless you believe that there is a "point of total convergence" at the root of you where you *are* (not *can* be, or "dear Lord help me to be") created in the image-likeness of God, the Christ, the son of the living God. Meditation is not the means of painting your inner self with a gilding of divinity. It is, rather, the gentle call to "awake thou that sleepest," to realize and release the Allness of love, and to "open out a way whence the imprisoned splendor may escape."⁶

At the very root and center of you, there is only God, which means there is a point in you where you are only God. "Be still," says the Psalmist, "and know that I AM God" (46:10). Meditation is the "be still and know." And since we are told that "God is love," this knowing can be, should be, an affirmation of love—leading to its feeling and acceptance. At the Center where there is only God, who is love, I am God and I am love. It is this knowing that God is and I AM which brings us into a consciousness of "total synthesis." This is the great love affair with God. This is pure meditation. It has no object, seeks no experience, desires no thing, works for no demonstration. It does not even try to create oneness; it *is* Oneness, a great fusing of light at the Center, "the same light that lighteth every man coming into the world."

Now, as in all love experiences, there is an elevation of consciousness. Thus, because of your inward perception and feeling, everything in your world as revealed by your senses appears different. Jesus acknowledges this when He says, "Blessed are the pure in heart, for they shall see God" (Matt. 5:8). In elevation of consciousness one sees from a transcendent level, he sees from the consciousness of God, by which he sees the point of light at the center of all things and all persons.

Take a few moments for another exercise, an experience in seeing transcendentally. Look around you wherever you are. (It might be more effective if you are seated out of doors in a garden or park.) Fix your attention on a tree, a flower, a cloud, a bird, or a lonely person seated on a park bench. Get the feeling of that "inmost center" within you where you experience oneness with God's love. Feel the warmth of love flowing *through* you and from you. In this loving consciousness you are letting yourself be loved from within, and letting yourself BE love. And then—look lovingly upon the tree or flower or person. If you sit still enough and concentrate on *not* doing anything or even *trying* to see anything, you will suddenly sense and see in a way beyond sight a radiance of light in that object or person. You will feel a closeness with it that is not emotional or sensual. It will give rise to understanding, to friendliness, and to a total freedom from fear. This is the height of the Oriental "Namaskar" (the divinity in me salutes the divinity in you). In this consciousness there could be no conflict, no hurt or harm, no fear or bitterness. There could be only a kind of joining of what is deepest within that object or person. George Washington Carver meditated on the lowly peanut in this way and unlocked its secrets, bringing prosperity to the entire South. Dostoevsky says this practice of relating to all of nature with love will lead you to "perceive the divine mystery of things

. . . and you will come at last to love the whole world with an all-embracing love."[7]

Keep in mind that this love is not something that comes from you, something that is generated in you and by you. It is an energy force flowing through you from that Cosmic Center within you, and touching and igniting that same energy force within the object or person. Now we can see how the kind of thoughts that reveal an absence of love—fear, hatred, hostility, resentment, anger—frustrate this inner realization and flow of transcendental love, and cause us to relate to the object or person on a purely surface level that is exterior to this inner point of oneness of love.

This is why it is truly said that "perfect love casts out fear" and "love overcomes the world." Of course, this does not mean that simply voicing the words, "I love you," will establish this oneness. As someone once said, "I loved him all the way to the divorce court." This shows how the word "love" has so often been a cover-up for hypocrisy. It is not just affirming, "I know love can solve this inharmony between us, and I will love him even if it kills me." As we have been saying, love is not the plaything of the emotions or senses, but the activity of Divine Law.

The need is to turn from the conflict and "let the soul banish all that disturbs. . . ." And then "think of Spirit as shining in from all sides" while you just relax and be still. Let the emanations of the Cosmic point of Divine Love flow in and through you, lifting you to the feeling of BEing love, enabling you to think loving thoughts of the other person, and thus relate to that depth of love which is surely within him—no matter how he may have been frustrating it.

You may wonder, how can you know if your meditation has found true depth? We should come forth thinking kindlier thoughts, speaking gentler and more loving words, and we should find ourselves doing things that are loving and harmonious with no actual effort to do them. And there should be a sharpening of the sensitivities. Things everywhere should take on the kind of appearance that things have to the person who is in love. As Shakespeare puts it, you will find "tongues in trees, books in the running brooks, sermons in stones, and good in everything."[8] And it is this kind of seeing, this level of perception, that projects a healing energy to everything that your life touches.

We are not saying here that love is the only element of the inner life of man, or that meditation is purely a means of realizing and releasing love. We are saying that love is an excellent basis for meditation, and meditation is a most effective key to knowing and experiencing "inner-centered" love. And, as we are trying to impress upon you, meditation is *not* a fixed thing, with a fixed set of definitions, techniques, and roads to follow. It is an individual experience. No one can tell you how to find the Center in you, and no one can hold your hand and go with you. You are an individual in God, and thus you can only find inward communion by going alone. Of course, as we have said, you are never less alone than when you experience this kind of aloneness, for it is really *all oneness.*

Meditation is the path you cut for yourself while seeking to get beyond the limitations of human consciousness into the transcendence of spiritual unity. It is and must be a continuing adventure—and proficiency and progress in depth can only come through practice. You will blaze your own trail, create your own gospel, be your own teacher, and follow your own master, which is the God-self of you at the heart of you which is created in the image-likeness of God who is love.

How does this meditation process relate to what we have traditionally called prayer? It must be said that meditation is irrelevant to the old concept of duality, where prayer is reaching out and up to God, asking for things or for mercy. In the concept of *unity* in which the meditation process functions, prayer is a projection of a consciousness which must first be experienced. Meditation is the inward experience, the in-building, the recharging, the mobilizing of the energy. Prayer is the conditioning of outer things, experiences, relationships, by speaking the word of truth. Thus prayer should not be asking or begging, but affirmation and accepting—a kind of letting.

You may have a great desire to see a cessation of war and of "man's inhumanity to man" in the world. And you may have prayed long and hard for peace through years of religious practice. Perhaps now you can see in a totally new sense that love is the answer. How do you pray for great waves of love to sweep over the earth, healing and harmonizing and protecting all people? There is a popular song that says, "Let there

be peace on earth and let it begin with me." Many have sung this
without realizing what is implied. To truly pray for peace in the world,
we must find the Center of peace and love in ourselves. For what is peace
except the all-pervading activity and energy of love that unites people
in a way that completes and fulfills them, and joins them by what is
deepest in themselves. There is a consciousness of inner peace arising
out of the fullness of transcendental love. Prayer is the projection of this
realization out into the world of men and experience.

However, we can project only what we have or what we are. To pray
for world peace in the concern over war or in the feeling of fear and
insecurity or with a sense of revulsion at widespread injustice and crime
is to pray with empty vessels. In the old days a volunteer fire department
was composed of individuals who responded to the fire bell by joining
a bucket brigade that conveyed buckets of water to the fire from the
nearest water source. How futile would have been this process if each
volunteer fireman had picked up a bucket and raced to the fire to throw
his bucket of nothing on the fire. In this instance the bucket was useless
without the water with which to extinguish the fire. And the prayer of
words, no matter how fond the hopes or sincere the wishes of the one
who prays, is but a conveyance of empty buckets. Or, in the case of the
person praying in a great consciousness of fear or worry, the buckets
could even contain inflammable material that would heighten the fire.

Meditation is the key to the storehouse of power which prayer can
effectively project. As the fireman went first to the source of water, in
prayer we must go first to the depth of our inmost self, not to get the
power, but to realize that "I AM the power." Thus, meditation cannot
be a tense reaching for anything. It must be the immersion of ourselves
in the Allness of life in which we have true being. Meditation is not
trying to create oneness with God, or even to seek it as a "gift of God."
To *try* to effect oneness is to acknowledge twoness. It is simply going
deep within ourselves, away from the point where there appears to be
duality, to the point where oneness is all there is. Then, resting in that
oneness, feeling the fullness of love, which at this point is the only reality
of us, we are ready to speak the word of love.

However, now as we speak the word of love, remember "the word which you hear is not mine but the Father's who sent me" (John 14:24). The words of our prayer are no longer hopes or aspirations or the fervent supplication to God to do something for us or for the world. They are the pure projection of the thought of reality, which, in a sense, is not a projection of anything. It is the acceptance of a reality that is present at the Center of all persons and all things.

We have traditionally prayed *to* God *for* things. This is an idea that must be unlearned, a practice that must be changed. First we follow the ideal, "Be still and know that I AM God." We get the consciousness of oneness, the feeling of the Presence of Infinite Love and Life and Power which is present in us—and *as* us. This is meditation. And then we speak the word of truth. Praying, not *to* God, but *from* the consciousness *of* God. Praying, not to make things happen, but to accept them on a level beyond appearances where that which we seek is already done. "Before they call I will answer." Praying, not to change things or set them right, but to accept things and see them rightly.

If you would pray for peace in the world, or for harmony between men or nations, or for love in the lives of lonely or discouraged persons, turn from the condition and your great concern about it to find and feel your own point of oneness in God, your own awareness of the Allness of love. Dwell as constantly upon this as two lovers dwell in the feeling of mutual love and adoration. Celebrate the reality of you that is created in and of love. Know that you are *in* love with all God's creation and that all things are *in* love with you.

And then, when this whole experience becomes an unquestionable reality to you, your bucket is filled. You are ready to act on the fire. Speak the word. "Thou shalt also decree a thing, and it shall be established unto thee" (Job 22:28, ASV). Affirm: "I am *in* love with all men and nations, and they are *in* love with me. We are united in love on a level of Spirit and in this consciousness, 'I, if I be lifted up, will draw all men unto me.' And I now decree that all relationships between all men and all nations are on this level of the oneness of love."

Practice the presence of God who is love, in the realization that the Presence is present in you as a depth of you. Pray much for the world and for any and all things that may concern you, but first of all heal your concern by turning within in meditation. "In the beginning . . . love!" The root of reality of you and of all the creation is love. And at this level of consciousness you are one with all the creation. At this point it is true that "I and my Father are one," and also "I am my brother and my brother is me."

Dwell often upon this feeling of oneness with the Father, and also in this consciousness of oneness in love with your brother. Then it will be true in a way that is dynamic and powerful, "Let there be peace on earth, and let it begin with me." It *will* begin with you, and go forth from you in waves of love energy, reaching out into all the world with the transcendent influence that will lead to a "union whose attainment is the only business of nature." And it will come about because of your own love affair with God, which is your only business in life.

9. *Love Claps Its Hands*

The paradox is that love is not only the key to abundant living and the fullness of joy, it is also the cause of much of man's unhappiness and misery. "The affairs of the heart" are intimately involved with much of what is tragic in human experience. Of course it is not love, but the perversion of love. But then this is what passes for love for most persons, and, as we have said, true love is a relatively rare phenomenon in our society.

We have been concerned in this work with the need to understand the nature of "inner-centered" or transcendental love. We have been repeating over and over that love is the foundation of the creative process, the root of the reality of the universe, and the very nature of the Infinite Power and Presence that we call God. God is love and man is created in God's image-likeness. Thus, man is created *in* and *of* love.

Love is not something that has come to some and has been withheld from others. We may have been thinking that our life lacks love because we were not loved by indifferent parents or because life has been unkind to us. But this is a "copout" and the sooner we realize it the closer we will come to the freedom we all secretly desire. Life's early experiences may have tended to frustrate our love, but there is just as much love within us as there was in Jesus, or Buddha, or St. Francis. We never lack love. We lack only the consciousness of the reality of our being.

How often we stray from the root of reality into the circumference of living. In dealing with the changing, challenging circumstances of every day we tend to forget who we are. We need to take time occasionally to affirm the truth that we are rooted and grounded in the Allness of love. The most important thing we can ever do is to "call to remembrance" our true nature, created in the image and likeness of God who is love. In the depths of us there is a silent voice that whispers interminably, "Awake thou that sleepest. Awake and remember who you are." And in the awakening and remembering comes the fullness of joy.

Recalling Jesus' parable of the Prodigal Son, joy is the wayward one "coming to himself." There is a sudden realization that he is out in the far country, cut off from all that is real. He has been seeking the things that he thinks will make his life meaningful. Suddenly he knows that meaning is not found in the world or in things, only in himself. Coming to himself is coming to the realization of his oneness with God and with all life.

Joy is the awareness that at the heart and root of us, regardless of outer circumstances, there is always enough love to go around. It is knowing that "He who is in you is greater than he who is in the world" (I John 4:4). This doesn't imply a personal God. It means a depth or consciousness of Allness. And the greatest consciousness of Allness is the consciousness of love. It means love, not as emotion or sentiment, not as something that happens between people, but as something that is forever happening between man and his Source. Joy, then, is the awareness of this depth in us, welling up and spilling over and "clapping its hands" in exuberant response to the vibration of the Symphony of Life.

The Psalmist sings, "Clap your hands, all peoples. Shout . . . with loud songs of joy!" (47:1). This is not a command to do something in an outer sense, in hopes that it will become real because we do it. It is, rather, an identification with the depth of us which is the reality of us, spilling over so that we can't restrain ourselves. We simply "clap our hands."

In religious meetings or services of worship it is not considered proper to applaud performances. Often, after a musical performance or a lecture or sermon, we may find it difficult to restrain the impulse to "clap our hands." The reason for this urge is not primarily because we want to show our appreciation to the performer or speaker. That is secondary, and certainly a very gracious thing to do. But the primary reason for the

compulsion to applaud is that we have been moved through the experience to touch the reality at the depth of us. It wells up and overflows
so that it is hard to contain.

This is an insight into the dynamic of transcendental love and how
when we experience the sense of oneness, love flows forth and "claps its
hands" in the spontaneous feeling of joy. It helps us to realize that
happiness is not a reactionary emotion, but an emanation of an inner
experience of communion. It could be said that the quest for happiness
is one of the chief sources of unhappiness, because we are looking in the
wrong direction.

The American Declaration of Independence, prized document that
it is, has one serious flaw. It talks of the inalienable right to "life, liberty,
and the pursuit of happiness." To think of "life" and "liberty" as rights
is to assume that they are things to be discovered and conquered or
demanded. Paul says, "The free gift of God is eternal life" (Rom. 6:23).
Life is innate and constant. It is not a right to be claimed, but a reality
to be accepted and lived. And it is in the living of life that we know
freedom. Rousseau says, "Man is born free; and everywhere he is in
chains."[1] His chains are imposed by the frustration of his own potentiality. They are made fast by his resistance and bitterness, which dams up
the flow of love. There is no greater bondage than the restriction of love,
and no greater freedom than the full experience of "inner-centered
love."

However, the greatest "flaw" in this great document is in the idea of
the "pursuit of happiness." It is encouragement to go out into the far
country, like the Prodigal Son, in quest of the things that will bring
meaning and happiness. This is the great delusion that plagues the lives
of most persons. It may be the very cause of the overemphasis upon
materialism in our "American way of life."

We say, "When this or that happens—then I will be happy." "When
I get that raise in salary, or the new mink coat, or when the children
are through college, or when the bills are paid—then I will be happy."
It is like Little Jack Horner who stuck in his thumb and pulled out a
plum, our lives are forever dependent for happiness on the "plums" we
come by. But this "thumb-plum" concept leads to life on the deferment

plan. The fullness of life is always just around the corner in the better job or the promotion or that retirement "sungalow" in Florida.

The "American Dream" for most persons is the dream of affluence, of achieving a level of life that may include a home in suburbia with two cars in the garage and complete with TV-hi-fi console and all the appliances to make living "gracious." And the dream is often fulfilled; for more than any other culture in the history of mankind, modern Americans have achieved a modicum of affluence. But the price has been high; perhaps beyond our spiritual means. We have gloried in the "right" to pursue happiness. But pursuing is not finding or experiencing, and it may be true that Americans are among the most unhappy people in the world. We may well be far ahead of the rest of the world in the achievement of the kind of things that we thought would bring happiness. However, joy can never come through self-indulgence, only through self-realization.

When we live by the premise that happiness comes only through a flow of good things and experiences, then it follows as night the day that an absence of what we have called good leads to unhappiness. Recently a woman remarked on returning from a trip through a primitive section of the world, "How unhappy those people must be. Why, they don't even have television!" And we see this principle in an even sharper focus in the story of the monarch who was facing a prolonged siege of depression. His advisers told him to find a truly happy man and wear his shirt for a week and this would alter his consciousness. So the king sent his emissaries out into the kingdom to search for the happy man. Weeks passed with reports coming back that they could not find a really happy man. Finally the report came that they had found the man who was truly happy, but alas, he didn't have a shirt to his back.

Somewhere I read an account of a man having dinner in a large restaurant on Times Square right after the second World War, when soldiers were coming home and there was an air of celebration everywhere. Seated by his table were four young persons, two soldiers in uniform and two girls, noisily making merry. As he gazed at one of the soldiers and listened to his brave young laughter, a great lump grew in his throat. He was blind!

The man began to think of how much this lad had given to his country, to those who enjoy it and reap its privileges. He felt that he should go to the boy and bow humbly before him and tell him how grateful he was and how he shared his hurt. He wanted to tell the young man how sorry he was that he could not see the lovely girl who sat across from him, smiling ardently at him. How could he do it? And then in a flash of insight the question changed to "Why should I do it?" The young man was obviously happy. It is not fitting to say to a happy person, "I am sorry that you are not happier."

The man suddenly realized that his values were faulty. He had equated happiness with the things that we usually assume are required to make us happy. But nothing really makes us happy, and nothing can really make us unhappy. We are always as happy as we make up our mind to be. This young man had faced his crisis successfully. In the furnace of his affliction he had forged a solid base of oneness at the heart of him. On this foundation of supportive love, he had the calm assurance that he was equal to any and all experiences in life. He knew that within him was the unborn possibility of the overflow of love and that he had the privilege at any time or place and under any circumstance of giving birth to it. As this overflow of love "clapped its hands" through him in a spirit of joy, it is obvious that he was seeing a reality in life that most persons do not see. As the Blind Ploughman sang, "I thank God that life has taken away my eyes that my soul might see."

Now it is not at all that there is anything wrong with things. We live in a prodigal universe, and there is a legitimate, royal abundance for all. It is a matter of priorities. What is the goal of life? If we set our goal at having things, then we will have at the *expense* of our being, and we will come to know a deep inner want that no outer thing or experience can satisfy. But if we seek chiefly to BE, then out of the fullness of BEING will come a glorious release of creativity. We will have the things too, but they will come out of the *expanse* of our BEING.

This is why Jesus said, "Seek first his kingdom . . . and all these things shall be yours as well" (Matt. 6:33). Seek first the realization of oneness —with God and with all life. Out of this consciousness will inexorably flow the attracting energy of love, which will draw to us right relationships, abundant supply, and harmonious experiences. Life is not just a static experience involving persons and jobs and houses and money. It is a dynamic unfoldment of the expanding possibilities of the creative process. This is what the Kingdom of Heaven is. The very word "heaven" comes from the Greek root word, *ouranos*, which means "expanding."

Jesus also said, "It is your Father's good pleasure to give you the kingdom" (Luke 12:32). When our chief motivation in life is to be a part of the joyous process of unfolding the potential that we are, then we find ourselves in tune with "the Father's good pleasure." His joy in unfolding the abundance of life suddenly becomes our joy in accepting and sharing it.

In trying to describe or define this elusive "kingdom," Jesus said it was like unto a seed that was planted in the ground and grew and brought forth plenty. The power of the seed is in its self-acceptance. A seed doesn't worry about who it is nor try to be something other than what it is. The joy of the seed is in knowing, "I am a seed." It doesn't "toil or spin or gather into barns." It is simply engaged in BEing. And out of the fullness of BEing, which is a fullness of joy, it gives birth to a continuity of seeds and harvests and future sowings.

"The Kingdom of God is within you" (Luke 17:20, ASV). This is one of the most reassuring ideas ever given to man. Within you is *where it's at!* And joy is the fullness of the inner Kingdom, which is your dynamic potentiality for growth. There can be no fear or anxiety when we know our oneness with this Kingdom of all good. Victor Hugo refers to this when he describes the bird that pauses for awhile on bows too slight, and yet sings, knowing he has wings. Can't you see the bird sitting there with the frail twig bouncing up and down. He is totally oblivious of any danger. He is singing his heart out because he knows who he is. His song is a song of self-realization.

There is no greater joy than the joy of knowing I AM. When you know that you are created in and of love, there is the joy of knowing I AM LOVE—and I am "loveful." Thus, like the bird resting on a shaky twig confident of his wings, when you find yourself in a difficult experience where there is hostility or anger or injustice, you can still sing with joy in the awareness that you are *in* love with all persons and there is enough love to go around.

The singing of the bird is actually an overflow of the Symphony of Life. His singing demonstrates that he is completely in tune with the unity of the whole creation. And Victor Hugo says, "be like this bird." God is singing a song through you—the melody and rhythm of your life. It is a song of love, for how could God sing of anything else? As you let this melody sing itself through you, the pattern of your life becomes varied, innovative, beautiful, interesting, and creative, and it is in all ways *you!* You are completely in harmony with the whole of creation. There is no competition, no strain, no fear that someone else will sing your song or take away what is yours.

Every morning of your life you awaken to a new day. When you look out upon the world revealed by the dawn, you face one of Life's great crises. It is interesting that in its translation into the more complicated Chinese language the word "crisis" is defined by two words: "danger" plus "opportunity." Viewing the new day in the morning is dangerous because of the appearance of things. The weather report, the stock market returns, the news of the day, and the ominous moods of your associates may indicate that your world is in a precarious condition. It is a threat to your security and stability. If you are living by the "thumb-plum" concept, there are no apparent plums and thus it is a dark day.

However, your first view of the day is an opportunity to look with eyes of love, to see things from a consciousness of oneness, and to let this transcendent awareness of the Cosmic energy of love well up within you and pour forth through you to "clap its hands" in joy. You literally applaud the world for all the good that you know is on the way despite appearances to the contrary.

It is a beautiful way of life, facing the crisis of the dawn by accepting the opportunity instead of the danger of it. In this consciousness you begin each day by tuning in to, and turning on, the "Symphony of Life." You refuse to let your day be determined by dark clouds on the horizon, or your consciousness influenced by the doleful preachments of "these troubled times." In all the history of civilization there have always been gloomcasters prating of the imminent fall of civilization. Praise God there have also been those who have looked through the darkness of despair to sing that "God's in His heaven—all's right with the world!" and to proclaim, "To be alive in such an age!"

Take some time at the beginning of the day to be still in quiet meditation, to indulge your "love affair with God." The Psalmist sings, "I will sing a new song to thee O God" (144:9). This is the song of your soul which God is singing through you. It is your personal "mantra," the vibrational pattern of life that is in focus *as* you. Listen and rejoice, and then declare, "God has put a new song in my heart and I sing for joy." That day will be a joyful day and a harmonious and successful day when you tune out the song of other days and tune in on the song that the Infinite is singing in you and *as* you in that moment.

Of course the next crisis you will face is when you walk into your office or shop, happy and singing and figuratively clapping your hands with joy. Those who have accepted the danger of the day's crisis will say, "What's wrong with you? What do you have to be so happy about?" Obviously you will need to employ restraint in the manner in which you outwardly express your exuberance and the overflow of love. But the beautiful part of it is the realization that you never need to have things to be happy about. You can be happy if you make up your mind to be so, and if you seek to know and unfold the inner Kingdom of creative love. That person who asks what you have to be so happy about reveals by his question that he "has eyes but sees not, and ears but hears not." He has never really seen the sunrise or sunset. He has never really experienced the fullness of love. His life is a ceaseless quest for love, for meaning, for happiness, and for the things that he thinks will bring fulfillment. He takes trips around the world to see things, but he takes his empty self wherever he goes; thus he sees from that consciousness of emptiness. He journeys to the Holy Land and returns to report that there were fleas in his room. He attends the Oberammergau Passion Play and announces only that the food was bad.

You do not need to have anything to be happy about! When you are conscious that you are *in* love with life, with all God's creation, and that the whole universe is *in* love with you, you have everything going for you. You have the sense that you are "destiny's darling," that there are green lights wherever you look. This consciousness wells up from within you and you clap your hands with joy from the overflow. It isn't a case of what you have to be happy *about*. It is more a matter of what you are happy *from*. Your happiness is the extension of an unfolding process out of the depths within. In a way you are happy because you *are* happy. The happiness is its own reason and its own cause.

One woman made the great discovery of her innate joy potential, and it came as a healing wellspring for her. She had been sick, weighed down by a sense of responsibility that she felt unable to meet, filled with troubles and heavy with discouragement. She chanced to read an article which contained the sentence, "Until you are happy you will be neither healthy nor free." The words leaped out at her. She angrily objected: "But how can I be happy when I have such trouble and so much pain?" But the words kept running through her mind.

Because she was so tormented by doubts, irritations, and frustrations, and because she had the restless urge to be "up and doing," she somewhat skeptically decided to try, Pollyanna-like, to "be happy." It was a puzzling thing—not being happy about something, but being happy for happiness' own sake.

Gradually it dawned on the woman that, bound up somehow with the paramount issue of spiritual faith—and material rewards—was the equally important issue of improving her own disposition. She recalled a statement from Henry Drummond, "Life is full of opportunities for learning love. The world is not a playground, it is a schoolroom. Life is not a holiday but an education, and the one eternal lesson for all of us is how better we can love."[2] It was not easy, but gradually she discovered a deeper potential for love within herself, and the ability to think lovingly about the persons and experiences that she had assumed to be the cause of her present dilemma. She began to live more calmly; to see life more clearly and in better proportion.

And then one day she made the great discovery of "In the beginning . . . love." She had been thinking about love, pondering the idea that it is not the plaything of human volition, but the action of divine law. Suddenly it was as if she were a spectator at the Creation. God who was totally the Presence and Power of love began to form and shape things out of himself. *He had nothing with which to work except love.* All things were formed out of this creative essence of love. She realized that this meant that she, too, had been created *in* and *of* love. What a thrilling discovery! "In the beginning, God" now became more meaningful to her as "In the beginning . . . love!" In a very real sense the transcendent energy of love was now and always the very root of her being and the source of her limitless potential for becoming. It was such a moving experience, just knowing this, that she found herself bursting forth in exuberant singing. Her face was aglow with the air and the smile of joy. In a figurative sense (and perhaps literally, too), love clapped its hands through her.

After this, and with very little reason outwardly to justify it, she was happy—totally and completely happy. And the happier she felt, the more strong and healthy and positive she became, giving even more reasons for happiness. And as her joy increased, her disposition improved, her strength gradually returned, and before long she had totally and completely recovered in all ways.

The dramatic transformation experienced by this woman started the moment she realized that "until you are happy you will be neither healthy nor free." The world would call this Pollyanna. But by whatever name we call it, this woman found that when we touch the root of reality within us and experience the flow of inner-centered love, we have the whole universe on our side. It may appear that we have lifted ourself by the bootstraps. More realistically, we are being lifted by the continuing creative process that made the bootstraps (and us) in the first place.

Perhaps we have misjudged Pollyanna, the unusual little-girl creation of novelist Eleanor Hodgman Porter. Pollyanna knew that nothing can *make* you happy, but anything can provide you with the opportunity to be happy if you want to be happy—and she simply wanted to be happy. She found gladness in things that meant only dismay to other people. When an automobile ran her down and injured her, she found cause for gladness in the fact that her convalescence gave her a good chance for reading and gave her a new slant on life. Unfortunately, Pollyanna has been given the connotation of the weak, insipid, and completely impractical attitude of extreme and unfounded optimism. This, because we have not understood that "the Kingdom of God is within," is an unborn possibility of love and joy which we can give birth to at any time.

If this is Pollyanna, then perhaps Jesus was the greatest Pollyanna of all time. He talked about a "wellspring" within man, from which he could draw all that he needed at any time to make his life abundant. He knew that most persons are exteriorly oriented, looking outside themselves for all things—and especially for happiness. His whole mission was to help people to turn inward and discover the new world of their infinite potential. He said, "These things I have spoken to you, that my joy may be in you, and that your joy may be full" (John 15:11).

Jesus was a doer. His gospel is replete with commands to "go," "do," "seek," "stretch forward," etc. Life is a constant unfoldment, and joy is the very happening of life. Actually, it is the overflow of love in the process of BEing. There can be no joy in stagnation or static existence. This is why we have suggested the move from "love" to "loving." Love may be only a concept, while loving is a creative happening.

The word "happiness" comes from the word "happen." Man is a creative being, the focus of an Infinite Idea being unfolded by a creative process. When man is in tune, things happen. Songs are composed, houses are built, cakes are baked, and books are written. All creative things come out of the overflow of this Infinite process. Since man is a creature of love there is a love energy that is basic to the creative flow. When he is consciously *in* love with life, there is a spilling over of creativity and in this overflow love "claps its hands" in a boundless demonstration of good and an experience of abounding joy.

The key to the continuity of joy in life is to let life happen. We live in a world of change. There is little point in trying to hold back the tides, and thus to resist the relentless process of growth and change. He who resists change resists life's happening. He holds back. He resists. Out of a faulty self-image he rejects life's fullness. Through unworthiness he settles for less than the best, and thus he impedes the flow of good. The problem is in his attempt to "unhappen" things, which leads to unhappiness. We must learn to let the creative flow unfold. Happiness is in the letting. Whenever we frustrate the letting process, or in guilt or regret try to "unhappen" something that has already manifest, we inhibit the bubbling forth of joy.

The healthy-minded person, one who is grounded in an awareness of oneness with the creative process of love within him, meets the experiences of life with nonresistance. He lets life happen, and then he can deal with the pain or sorrow or injustice that may result, seeing it all as a growth experience. But not so the unhealthy-minded one. He sees things from the "thumb-plum" perspective, and he hasn't had many plums lately. Life for him seems to be the constant happening of persons and situations that are a threat to him. He has no sense of security in himself. He does not know his I AMness. He does not feel the fullness of love in his heart. So, if people do not stay put, he feels disturbed and threatened. He aggressively tries to "unhappen" them, to make them over as he thinks they should be. He is like a spectator at a play who accepts the scenery of the first scene, and then wrestles with the stagehands to prevent them from changing the scenery as the play unfolds. It is probably true that most of the unhappiness that man experiences is the result of this subtle attempt to "unhappen" things and people.

The healthy-minded person is in tune with the flow, like a dancer moving with the stirring music of a square dance, changing partners, moving to all parts of the floor, but secure because he is in tune and in time with the music. One wonderful woman, old in years but youthful in spirit, has that exuberant and adventuresome temperament that is always so refreshing to behold. She says, "I just hate to think of dying —not that I fear death—but life is such an interesting motion picture story, I just can't bear to think of not waking up in the morning to see what comes next." This is a happy person, because she keeps nonresistantly in tune with life's happening.

It is resistance to life's happening that causes so much unhappiness among people in retirement. These people have come to a point of chronological age that the world has adjudged as "too old" for work or productivity. How often there is an unconscious attempt to "unhappen" the years, to "unhappen" the actual retirement from work or the separation from family and friends.

Why try to change life's happening? Your age is what it is, and it is good. As Browning says, "Grow old along with me! . . . The last of life, for which the first was made."[3] Age is not a limited thing at all. Gerald Heard calls it "second maturity." It is a new opportunity to set fresh goals, to launch into new projects. Don't try to unhappen what has happened. Accept it. Rejoice in it. Change your retirement to an "advancement." Think of your new experience in terms that spell dynamic living rather than static existence. But at all costs face forward with the joyous sense that life *is* happening, and not *has* happened.

Wherever we are in life and whatever may be our age, the joy of life is the joy of going on. At nine or ninety, we can still live but one day at a time. We are still confronted each morning with the choice of whether to sing the new song of life or "harp on the same old tune." Whether we are old or truly youthful depends not on chronological age but on the conscious choices we make at the beginning of every day and in meeting the changes all through the day. Regardless of state or station or time of life, the unhappy persons are those who try to "unhappen" things. And the happy ones are those who face the future calm and unafraid and with nonresistance, singing the new song of today. Joy is going onward in faith, cheered on by an inner support of love clapping its hands.

In the nativity story the angels sang a song of joy as they heralded the birth of Jesus. It was to be a "sign unto us" of the ultimate birth of the God-man in all of us. We are told that this will come "as a thief in the night." In other words, it may happen suddenly at any time and many times. And this is the fullness of joy, when, in the midst of a challenging experience, we come to ourselves and let the Christ out; release our "imprisoned splendor"; and let the fullness of our God-self become the reality of our experience.

However, let us make clear that we are not dealing with the whim of a divine being but with the inexorable activity of divine law. When Jesus said, "Ye shall know the Truth, and the Truth shall make you free" (John 8:32, ASV), He was saying, in effect, "If you open the doors and windows of your mountain cabin, you will have fresh air and light, just as when it was boarded up the interior was dark and musty. There is a distinct cause and effect." Knowing this . . .

Can you accept the truth that "it is your Father's good pleasure to give you the kingdom" (Luke 12:32) and not fulfill the promise: "I will . . . open you the windows of heaven, and pour you out a blessing, that there shall not be room enough to receive it"? (Mal. 3:10, ASV).

Can you accept the Truth that you are a child of God, created in His image-likeness, endowed with infinite possibilities, and not be joyful?

Can you accept the truth of "In the beginning . . . love!"; that you are created *in* and *of* love; and that love is the reality of your being— and not feel loveful"?

Know the truth, identify with your eternal oneness at the Center of you, and in that moment there will be a great exhilaration, for joy is love clapping its hands in the ecstasy of life's fullness. It is love rejoicing in the richness of the overflow. It is being *in* love with the Christ of you, and "Christ in you your hope of glory" being *in* love with you. It is knowing that you are a *loveful* creature, fully capable of meeting every changing situation, knowing that there is always enough love to go around.

*   *   *

Life is For Loving is not a book for frivolous reading. It is intended to challenge you to deeper study and meditation. Reread the book, talk back to it, and let it talk further with you in a kind of inner dialogue. I am concerned, not just that you understand and accept the ideas shared here, but that you understand and accept yourself.

And now, as you reminisce in the "afterglow" of this reading, recall that love is not an emotion, not sentimentality, not a sensual or sexual experience; but that it may use any or all of these as a conduit through which it flows in the process of communion of two whole persons—while the communion itself is or should be a transcendental experience. Remember: that love is the nature of the Presence of God and of you in whom it is present; and that the great need in life is to be loved (but you can only be loved from within. This is true security, since we are told, "Behold, I have loved you with an everlasting love.") And now, not with praise or appreciation of the book or its author but just as a means of symbolizing the spilling over of this love through you, *clap your hands for joy!*

Notes

Unless otherwise indicated, all Scripture quotations are from the Revised Standard Version of the Bible, copyright 1952 by Thomas Nelson & Sons.

1. From Love to Loving

1. St. Augustine, *The Confessions of Saint Augustine* (New York: Citadel Press, 1943), p. 41.
2. William Shakespeare, "Sonnet 116," *The Complete Works of William Shakespeare* (New York: Random House, 1952), p. 328.
3. Dostoevsky, *The Brothers Karamazov*, Vol. 12, Great Books of the Western World (Chicago: Encyclopaedia Brittanica, 1952), p. 167.

2. Love and Forgiveness

1. Robert Browning, "Paracelsus," Part 1, from *Masterpieces of Religious Verse* (New York: Harper & Row, 1948), p. 431.
2. Levi, *"Aquarian Gospel of Jesus Christ"* (Los Angeles: Leo Dowling, 1907), chap. 8, v. 21; chap. 39, v. 18.
3. *The Complete Writings of Ralph Waldo Emerson* (New York: William H. Wise, 1929), p. 148.

3. From Loneliness to Oneness

1. Thomas Wolfe, *Look Homeward Angel* (New York: Charles Scribner's Sons, 1947), from the Foreword.
2. Kahlil Gibran, *The Prophet* (New York: Alfred A. Knopf, 1952), p. 19.

3. St. Augustine, *The Confessions of Saint Augustine* (New York: Citadel Press, 1943), p. 1.
4. Arthur Miller, *Death of a Salesman, Arthur Miller's Collected Plays* (New York: The Viking Press, 1957), p. 146.
5. Anne Morrow Lindbergh, *Gift from the Sea* (New York: New American Library of World Literature, Signet Books, 1955), p. 49.
6. Erich Fromm, *The Art of Loving* (New York: Harper & Row, 1956), p. 46.

4. What God Hath Joined

1. Kahlil Gibran, *The Prophet* (New York: Alfred A. Knopf, 1952), p. 60.

5. Love and Sex

1. Murray Schisgal, *LUV* (New York: Coward-McCann, 1965), Preface.
2. William Shakespeare, *Merchant of Venice*, Act II, Sc. vi, line 36, *The Complete Works of William Shakespeare* (New York: Random House, 1952), p. 233.

6. The Healing Power of Love

1. Eric Butterworth, *Unity of All Life* (New York: Harper & Row, 1969), p. 158.

7. The Work of Your Life

1. Kahlil Gibran, *The Prophet* (New York: Alfred A. Knopf, 1952), p. 30.
2. *Ibid.* p. 31.
3. *Ibid.* p. 33.
4. George Eliot, "Stradivarius," from *John Bartlett, Familiar Quotations*, 14th Edition (Boston: Little, Brown & Co., 1968), p. 689.
5. Kahlil Gibran, op. cit., p. 30.

8. Man's Love Affair With God

1. Pierre Teilhard de Chardin, *Building the Earth* (Wilkes-Barre: Dimension Books, Inc., 1965), p. 45.
2. *Ibid.* p. 93.
3. Charles Fillmore, *Christian Healing* (Kansas City, Mo.: Unity School of Christianity, 1947), p. 132.

100 Life is for Loving

4. Teilhard de Chardin, *The Divine Milieu* (New York: Harper & Row, Harper Torchbooks edition, 1960), p. 112.
5. Charles Fillmore, *Keep a True Lent* (Kansas City, Mo.: Unity School of Christianity, 1953), p. 43.
6. Robert Browning, "Paracelus," Part 1, from *Masterpieces of Religious Verse* (New York: Harper & Row, 1948), p. 431.
7. Dostoevsky, *The Brothers Karamazov*, Vol 12, Great Books of the Western World (Chicago: Encyclopaedia Brittanica, 1952), p. 167.
8. William Shakespeare, *As You Like It*, Act 2, Sc. 1, *The Complete Works of William Shakespeare* (New York: Random House, 1952), p. 260.

9. Love Claps Its Hands

1. Jean Jacques Rousseau, *The Social Contract*, Vol. 38, Great Books of the Western World (Chicago: Encyclopaedia Brittanica, 1952), p. 387.
2. Henry Drummond, *The Greatest Thing in the World* (London: Collins, 1930), p. 37.
3. Robert Browning, "Rabbi Ben Ezra," from *Masterpieces of Religious Verse* (New York: Harper & Row, 1948), p. 77.

75 76 77 9 8 7 6 5 4